STEAL FROM YOUR HEROES

Pasteur Tran

Copyright © 2020 by Pasteur Tran

mail@passytee.com
www.passytee.com

All rights reserved. No part of this publication may be reproduced, stored in retrieval system, copied in any form or by any means, electronic, mechanical, photocopying, recording or otherwise transmitted without written permission from the publisher. You must not circulate this book in any format.

ISBN: 978-0-6489135-1-1 (paperback)
ISBN: 978-0-6489135-0-4 (ebook)

The right of Pasteur Tran to be identified as author of this work has been asserted by him in accordance with sections 77 and 78 of the Copyright, Designs and Patents Act 1988.

Cover design by Adam Renvoize
Formatting by Polgarus Studio

Printed in the United States of America
First Edition

Contents

1. STEAL FROM YOUR HEROES 1
2. CHANNEL THE HEROES 8
3. THE SECRET TO MOTIVATION 11
4. FAILURE IS GOOD 17
5. TAKE OWNERSHIP OF YOUR LIFE 22
6. PLAY WITH THE CARDS YOU ARE GIVEN 28
7. CHANGE COMES FROM WITHIN 34
8. SURROUND YOURSELF WITH RIGHT PEOPLE 34
9. ALWAYS LEARN 44
10. DON'T QUIT YOUR DAY JOB 49
11. FOLLOW YOUR INCLINATIONS 55
12. ALWAYS STAY CURIOUS 60
13. HAVE A CLEAR GOAL 65
14. CARVE YOUR OWN PATH 71
15. DO ONE THING DAMN WELL 76
16. SAY YES! 80
17. DON'T MISS THE BIG WAVES 84
18. GET TO THE POINT OF NO RETURN 89
19. DON'T HOLD GRUDGES 94
20. REJECTION IS A GOOD THING 99
21. IGNORE THE NOISE 105
22. BE RESPECTFUL 110
23. BECOME THE HERO 114

Acknowledgements 119
Bibliography 121

1. STEAL FROM YOUR HEROES

When you envision the success you wish to achieve, you probably have a hero who represents the epitome of success. You can almost see yourself standing where they now stand. You can almost taste the victories they have tasted. If you could steal just a fraction of their glory, wouldn't it be amazing?

But as you stare at those you look up to, have you considered how they got there? What obstacles they have faced? What sort of journey they went through to reach that pinnacle?

Richard Branson might be one of your heroes, but the philanthropy he is now known for is a result of his journey that made him who he is today. In fact, Branson even went to jail! More on that in a bit.

Warren Buffett reads voraciously now, but his rise to investment guru didn't allow him that luxury.

The hero's journey was critical to their success. Steal their methods, their ways of thinking, and the traits that led to their success. Steal what your heroes learned along the way.

Use a hero's success as the reference point to where you want to be.

Stephen King's success, for example, was not entirely his own. His first big hit, *Carrie* (his fourth novel but the first to be published) was due in part to his wife and is a great example of why you should surround yourself with people who support your goals. (The novel began as a short story, but King's wife encouraged him to turn it into a novel.)

If you want to be a successful entrepreneur, why not learn about Phil Knight, founder of Nike, or Peter Thiel, founder of PayPal? Even Mark Cuban can show you—despite the fact that his receptionist stole his company's money (a story discussed in detail later in this book)—how you can pick yourself up and become a billionaire in the process.

Choose your heroes carefully.

Choose those who achieved what you want to achieve.

Then, *steal* from them.

HOW TO FIND TRAITS

You can create the best version of yourself by hand-selecting the traits you most desire. Think of yourself as being made up of building blocks of traits. Think of the traits you want to acquire, and then hand pick which hero to steal them from to create who you want to be.

For example, if you want to be a writer, study the traits of your author heroes.

Take J. R. R. Tolkien and his first big success, *The Hobbit*. It was never going to be released, and only after one of Tolkien's students read a copy and contacted a publisher, did this book become published and bring about his success.

What Tolkien had was perseverance. He continued to work on his craft and write more books. He didn't write a book and place all his hopes on its success. Instead, he kept writing. Perseverance is a trait we can steal from Tolkien.

However, traits for becoming an author can be found in the lives of *other* heroes, so don't limit yourself just to heroes from just one specific area of expertise.

> *Heroes in different fields can teach you amazing traits that are universally beneficial.*

Many traits are universally helpful to your journey to success. Why not learn how to hustle, a trait necessary for starting any business, like Dale

Carnegie? Or Sam Zemurray, one of the most successful and powerful men of his time, who figured out how to make money by selling bananas?

There are many traits that can apply to different parts of your life. Steal them to use as building blocks for yourself. Steal them and make them work for *you*.

Within this book, I will go through the traits that are universal. These are traits you can apply to whatever your goal may be.

STEAL WHAT IS CONTROLLABLE

You can't control events and some events may never happen again. You can't steal them, nor should you try to. You *can*, however, control who you become and who you model yourself after. You will also have your own story. Every twist and turn will be unique, and taking advantage of events will be your path to achievements.

What we will steal in this book is how these heroes positioned themselves for future events and to understand what they did that was within their control to achieve success.

HEROES ARE HUMAN

When considering your heroes, you may find many to learn from (perhaps too many!), but most importantly, you will also realize that your heroes are human.

It's true that some people are simply born with a gift. Take a look at Mozart, who composed his first piano piece, "Minuet and Trio," when he was five years old! At that age some of us were simply trying to figure out how to open the fridge. Other heroes simply found their inclinations a lot earlier in their lives than most. In the end, however, they are like you and me. They have weaknesses.

Who would have thought Steve Jobs enjoyed LSD? Or that Andre Agassi likes to burn paper when he's stressed? Our heroes can also fail, let their emotions get the better of them, and sometimes they can result in costly mistakes.

Don't ever think that you can't be a hero. You steal to become one.

Heroes also have heroes and needed guidance. Everyone has someone they model themselves after. Jay Z had Russel Simmons. Warren Buffett had Benjamin Graham. Marcus Aurelius mentioned a whole list of people (his father, caretaker, etc.) in the first chapter of his book, *Meditations*. The list goes on and on.

Each of these heroes needed a point of reference.
To be a hero is to have your own heroes.

LEARN FROM THE MISTAKES OF HEROES

Are there bad and good heroes? You can learn a lot from "bad" people (or people with bad habits), as much as good ones.

Consider Nikola Tesla, a prolific man who discovered alternating current electricity. Did you know that in his early years, he was addicted to gambling? He was only able to quit after his mother gave him all of his family's savings, saying that he might as well spend all of it on his gambling addiction. He quit that very day. This is a gentle reminder that your heroes are human and can sometimes do odd and weird things.

If you don't need it, don't steal it. There is no good or bad.
Take only what you need and leave the rest.

When you steal from your heroes, take all the positive traits that you believe will suit you. Don't ignore the negatives though because you may be able to learn from them as well.

The important thing to learn is *how* they made the mistakes or *how* they treated people the wrong way that resulted in their failures. That is a free lesson for you.

You not only steal traits, but you also steal the lessons these heroes overcame. You get to see the result of a failure, without failing yourself. Learn from it and take it as yours.

Ultimately, there is no good or bad. There can only be positives and more positives. Be selective. Take the best traits for yourself. Ignore the harmful vices you don't want—but learn from them. That's the power of stealing from your heroes.

Just take everything that suits you in achieving your potential and goals. Create the profile that you want.

Everything you choose is a building block. Each piece you add gets you closer to the person you want to be as you build the best version of you.

ABUNDANCE

There is so much information out there for us to steal, but not everyone takes advantage of it. Why not?

It could be laziness. It could be not knowing who your heroes are. Or it could be the fact that biographies are so damn huge that no one has the time to extract the one paragraph that could change their life. But if everyone made that effort, there would be a lot of achievers out there. Yep, everyone would be rich and extremely happy—or both.

In a time when there are so many ways to access knowledge, we seem to find fewer people accessing what can help them. Too many distractions. Too many options.

Now is your time to give yourself an advantage. While everyone else is twiddling their thumbs, *you* steal the lessons, *you* learn, *you* get ahead.

Use this book as a template for creating who you want to be. Steal from me, as I have stolen from other heroes. The purpose of this book is to show you traits for your success. I will show you stories I have stolen and kept. Some of these heroes are very famous, some completely unknown. The facts may be surprising to you—I hope they are.

In the biography section at the end of the book, I reference each of my heroes. If you're interested in them, take the time to study and analyze them, since I have only given what was, for me, the essence of their stories that resonated with me—and *might* resonate with you.

I have organized this book according to overlapping traits that I believe are universal to success. Multiple heroes demonstrate them.

I have kept this book tight and to the point, as you mustn't just be reading. You must *do*!

Now, let's start stealing…

2. CHANNEL THE HEROES

I recall a time when I was about to speak in front of a crowd of a hundred people and found myself gripped by fear. But I remembered that many heroes have performed for much larger crowds. Tony Robbins speaks in front of thousands. Warren Buffett has a fear of talking to crowds yet holds huge annual shareholder meetings.

No matter their fears, they still get up and talk.

When I think of these moments, I realize that heroes face difficult moments in their life and yet still endure. They face their fears. They take risks. Some voluntarily get laughed at. Kevin Hart will still stand in front of a crowd and do comedy, even if he completely bombed the day before.

If they can do it, why can't I?

When you remember the stories of these amazing people and their successes and failures, you realize that *you* can do it, too.

That day when a hundred people were waiting for me to speak to them, I happened to be thinking of Kevin Hart and his failures on stage. To this day I still can't believe someone would get up, under a spotlight, and try to make the crowd laugh. It would scare the crap out of me.

But, he did it every day. He got up in front of a crowd with confidence—and so can I.

I cracked a smile. Then they announced it was my turn to go up and talk. My fears faded, and I kept thinking about how my heroes still succeeded. Even when they failed. And even if this is the worst speech of my life, I'll still succeed.

EVERY MOMENT THERE IS A HERO

For every moment in your life there is a hero you can remember and steal from.

When I'm stuck with making a decision, I ask myself, What would Richard Branson do? If the opportunity I faced would give him a chance to make something new and exciting to him, he would dive in. So, that's what I should do: Steal his intent, his bravado, and his willingness to dive into something new.

When I get rejected, I remember Jeff Bezos or Stephen King. They were rejected, but still pursued their vision and achieved it. Did they stop? No. Did it faze them? Not one bit. They just kept going.

> *To channel your hero is to think of them in the present moment. What would they do now? Then, do it.*

There are moments that will always stick out to you and resonate with you. Those are the moments you must channel.

I could easily tell you that Kobe Bryant has made multiple game-winning shots, but channeling that energy when he makes a shot doesn't help me much. However, I *do* remember when he *missed* a game-winning shot (yes, this has happened).

I'm reminded that every time he has the ball, he knows he may fail while at the same time knowing he will do his very best to put that ball in the basket. So, at that moment he *must* believe he will succeed. His mind is clear.

As Kobe once famously said, "If you're afraid to fail, then you're probably going to fail."

Suddenly, all I can think of is Kobe's self-confidence and his decision to go straight to the NBA from high school. The sprained ankle that would almost stop him playing. The teams that support him to take the shot and sometimes miss.

Suddenly, my failures seem so small—and then I keep going. If Kobe can, if my heroes can, why can't I?

And so, why can't you?

Whatever situation is presented to you, ask yourself what would your hero do? Channel that person's trait and do it.

SHARE WHAT YOU KNOW

When you learn about your heroes, share your knowledge, the stories, the journeys, and the difficulties that have inspired and motivated you.

I have found that the more you share, the more that people around you become inspired—and the more you will be reminded of the lessons you have learned. The more you learn, the more easily you can channel your heroes.

When my friend told me about wanting to open her own cake business, I told her the story of Milton Hershey and Gordon Ramsay (heroes you will learn about in this book).

Within a few months after stealing from her heroes, she began training for and dedicating herself to baking (but still keeping her day job). She then opened a little store in Australia. She's enjoying every bit of it.

In this book, I will share the stories and moments I have stolen, so you can share them with others.

3. THE SECRET TO MOTIVATION

How do heroes continually stay motivated? How did J.K. Rowling continue work on her series of Harry Potter novels even after her first novel was rejected 12 times by publishers?

She believed in herself.

She searched endlessly for a publisher, and due to a twist of luck, *Harry Potter and the Sorcerer's Stone* ("Philosopher's Stone" in England) was published because the publisher's daughter loved the book and wanted to know what happened next.

And what drove Marilyn Monroe to keep pursuing a career in Hollywood, even though producers told her she was not meant for it? Why did Bear Grylls pursue the S.A.S. (Special Air Service) a second time, after failing a grueling first time?

When you study your heroes, you will find one thing in common: They believe in something. Something so important to them that they won't budge or flinch in their pursuit of it. If the world said no, they said too bad, I'm doing it anyway.

J.K. Rowling believed in Harry Potter. Marilyn Monroe believed in herself. Bear Grylls believed he could get into the S.A.S. These beliefs kept them going and kept them motivated.

Heroes refuse to take no for an answer. That is the core of their motivation.

BELIEF IS YOUR DRIVER

Belief is the most critical driver you need in pursuit of any goal. Heroes all have a strong belief in something. Martin Luther King, Jr., believed in abolishing segregation and racism. Kobe Bryant had faith he could get into the N.B.A.

When you really distill any hero down to the very core, you will find unwavering belief. Belief so strong they will stand by it until they die. At every corner of their journey they are tested to see if they really want it, to see if they really mean what they say. You will face your own tests of your belief. If you don't think you will pass an exam, you won't.

The first digital game I ever made was never completed. I never really believed I would be able to finish it. I coded as a hobby, and although I had the vision to make something, I never had a final product in mind. In a manner similar to thinking that you may not pass an exam, if you don't think you will finish a product, you won't.

So when the coding got tough, I just gave up. I lost my motivation. I had nothing to draw upon. No motivational video or book was going to pull me out of my slump.

And why was that?

Because I didn't believe I could do it. *Because motivation isn't enough; belief trumps all.*

I know it sounds like I ripped out some moral of the story from the movies. But if you don't believe in something, then how do you plan to face rejection? Backstabbing? Friends and family leaving? How can you go through adversity if you don't believe you can do it? You *must* believe in something. If you don't believe in your product, at least believe in yourself.

FROM ROCK BOTTOM

J.K. Rowling's belief in her ability to write was tested multiple times. While she was on a train to Manchester in England, she thought of her new story idea and main character, Harry Potter. While working as a secretary in London, she would write as much as she could in her free time. Not long after, her mother passed away, and she was stricken with depression. She almost gave up writing. She would travel to work in Portugal, have a short-lived marriage, and give birth to a child, Jessica. She continued on, but it was only getting harder. She believed she could write her story. Even after all these crushing events in her life, she remained motivated: She was going to finish that book.

She returned to England as a lone parent without a job and lived off government paychecks.

"I was the biggest failure I knew," she reflected.

It was a dark time, but she became determined to succeed in writing. It was where she felt she "truly belonged." At cafés and shops, she would write as much as she could while taking care of Jessica. She directed all her energies into the book. Beyond her daughter, it was the only thing that mattered to her.

When she finished the book, she submitted her manuscript to a publisher. When she heard back, it was a letter of rejection. Twelve rejections later, she began losing confidence, but still believed in her story.

One day, the editor for Bloomsburg Publishing read the script at lunch and noticed that his daughter enjoyed the book as well. In fact, his daughter enjoyed the book so much he decided to publish it.

Luck? Maybe. But success doesn't come to someone who gives up. "Rock bottom became the solid foundation on which I rebuilt my life," Rowling said, at the 2008 Harvard Commencement Exercises.

Today, Harry Potter is a worldwide phenomenon. The world kept telling her to give up, testing her again and again. But Rowling did not stop believing. She believed in Harry Potter so much she finished the book and even in the face of repeated rejections, kept on approaching publishers.

Rowling isn't the only person who believed in her work.

Mary Kay Ash believed in her ability to build a cosmetic company from scratch. It is why she bought the original cosmetic formulas from her family and put her life savings on the line.

Howard Shultz believed he could make Starbucks into a global phenomenon. It was why he was so adamant on getting a job there.

BELIEVE IN THE VISION

When Howard Schultz wanted to join Starbucks, he was told no. Back then, Starbucks had only five small stores, and while it was a small company at the time, Howard had an aggressive idea growth strategy for Starbucks. He knew he could make it bigger.

He spent more time with the owners to show his eagerness and willingness to learn more about the business, but surprisingly, they told him he was too disruptive and would not fit the mold there. Although their view seemed final, Howard called the owner and explained why they needed him.

Then, he waited. He eventually did get the job (and took a very substantial pay cut).

In the following years, he would help grow Starbucks.

In his autobiography, *Pour Your Heart into It*, Howard wrote, "In daily life, you get so much pressure from friends and family and colleagues, urging you to take the easy way… but when you really believe—in yourself and in your dream—you just have to do everything you possibly can to take control and make your vision a reality."

Howard believed in himself. He knew he had the vision and believed he could make it happen.

Even when Howard temporarily left Starbucks to test out a new concept, he felt he would return. His new concept was to add other drinks and pastries. The owners told him Starbucks would not get into the "restaurant business."

So, what did Howard do? He set off on his own venture and opened Il Giornale, a store based on the premise Howard believed Starbucks should have been.

When Starbucks was up for sale, Howard jumped in and implemented his vision. It was successful and the company grew. Although all the signs were telling him to leave Starbucks for good, he just kept believing. That, at the very core, kept him motivated.

The world told him "no" yet he kept believing.

When he successfully opened a café to show the owners that Starbucks should offer other traditional espresso beverages, they said no. When Starbucks needed funding, he was continually told no (217 times, in fact).

But he kept going. He *believed* he could make Starbucks a worldwide phenomenon. Even when people told him to give up, he never did.

Howard would eventually become C.E.O. and Chairman of Starbucks, and aggressively expanded the company. If doors weren't opening for him, he would find another door. The belief remained the same—how he got there would change.

You must believe in your strengths. What you have learned, cultivated, or are confident in is something in which you should be proud.

Look at Rafa Nadal, who was told he had a genetic condition, Tarsal Scaphoid, which would prevent him from playing tennis. That didn't stop him. He was determined to be a grand slam winner. While in crutches, he would continue hitting tennis balls to his coach on the tennis court. He searched for someone to make unique shoes to accommodate his condition. Fortunately, he would find the shoes he needed and would eventually face off against Roger Federer—and win.

"I saw, more clearly than ever before, that the key to this game resides in the mind," said Nadal, in his book *Rafa: My Story*. "If your mind is clear and strong, you can overcome almost any obstacle, including pain. Mind can triumph over matter."

Or look at Kobe Bryant, who had unwavering confidence to join the N.B.A. at a young age. Having watched tapes of famous basketball players, and even playing against himself (he played against imaginary players), Kobe would continually work on his game. He spent hours doing drills, and while most people were on the playground, he was learning the fundamentals of basketball.

Although everyone told him he was not mature enough for pro basketball and should attend college, Kobe made a decision.

"I've decided to skip college and take my talent to the N.B.A.," he said, "and I know this is a big step, but I can do it. It's the opportunity of a lifetime. It's time to seize it while I'm young. I don't know if I can reach the stars or the moon. If I fall off the cliff, so be it."

Kobe believed in himself and that set him on a trajectory of success.

All these heroes believed in their strengths. They didn't doubt themselves. Even when quitting seemed like the most logical thing to do, they believed. That gave them the confidence and conviction to do what they wanted.

Are there times when you doubt yourself? When you don't believe in yourself? When something in the back of your mind convinces you that you can't do something?

Those are the times you must steal and channel your heroes to crush that voice.

When I find myself demotivated, I remind myself of my beliefs. I remind myself that I believe in achieving what I set out to do.

There will be people who pull you down. Some may convince you that you can't or shouldn't do something. Family members may tell you to stop. Friends may think your idea is stupid. All you will have left is your belief. When you feel that all is lost, belief is all you need to keep you going. The darkest of times will not stop you.

So, what *are* your beliefs? When you're determining what your next pursuit or goal is, how much do you believe in it? Do you believe in yourself and your ability to achieve it?

To stay motivated like your heroes, you must first convince yourself. If you're selling a product, you need to believe the product is the best thing in the world. If you're adamant on finishing your goals, you need to believe that you actually *will* get to the end.

You will not flinch when you're told it won't work. You will stand your ground because of your beliefs. Steal that conviction.

Whether the world tests you or other people question you, you must remain adamant in your belief and be motivated to get what you want.

Believing you can achieve your goals is the one element that will keep you motivated. Don't ever lose it. Keep believing.

4. FAILURE IS GOOD

Failure. It's a topic that's mentioned in every motivational book. Everyone experiences failure. It could be failing a business, failing an exam at university, or failing to win first place in a race. In a complete nutshell, it would make for a dull story: "Hero fails at something." She learns from it. She does it again. Maybe she still fails. But she does it again and again until she succeeds. That's it. That's how you beat failure. You learn from your previous mistakes and just keep going at it.

If one word were designated to that process, that word would be perseverance. Heroes persevere. They are stubborn. Failure doesn't stop them. It makes them want their dreams even more.

THE FAILURE OF A MOUSE

Walt Disney's journey is one of the best examples of a hero persevering after failing again and again. He never really had good luck as an artist, but he kept his dream and vision alive. When he decided to start an art studio with his friend, Ubbe Iwerks (nicknamed "Ub"), he would pay rent with his drawings because he had no money. A venture not making money is bound to fail and Disney's studio collapsed within a short time. But Disney didn't give up.

He believed he could make it as an artist.

He started a job at the Kansas City Film Ad Company, drawing and learning techniques in animation. When he felt he was financially stable, it was time to try once again.

Disney went on to found his second company, Laugh-O-Gram films. Although contracted for six short cartoons, less than a year later the company was nearing bankruptcy. Disney even had investors this time around. But in an unfortunate sequence of events, the company that had funded his six short cartoons was the first to go bankrupt. As a consequence, Laugh-O-Gram films followed.

It was a horrible time for Disney. He had absolutely nothing.

He would sleep at work, rent a bathtub to wash himself only *once* a week, and had a line of credit at a nearby restaurant.

The owner of the restaurant was getting annoyed with Disney because he wasn't paying. In anger, he stormed up and found Disney eating a cold can of beans, just to get enough nutrition.

"I was twenty-one years old. But I had failed," Disney says. "I think it's important to have a good hard failure when you are young."

When I heard this story, I was certain I would have given up on my dream. But not Disney.

Although he had lost almost everything, he was able to keep one of those six short cartoons. The film was called *Alice's Wonderland*. Sound familiar? You guessed it—with that single film he established another studio.

Third time's a charm.

He threw everything into making this effort succeed and paid the team far more than himself and directed all the profits into the studio. At that time, he met Charles Mintz, a producer who would provide additional work for Disney's new company. But, once again, the company was running low on money.

Disney requested more commission from Mintz. To his surprise, Mintz lowered his commission to ensure the company would fail. When Disney threatened to leave, Mintz was prepared.

"I'll ruin you," Mintz said. "I already have your key artists signed up." Disney hadn't realized Mintz had secretly lured all of his team members away. Mintz robbed Disney of everything.

Disney was pained to see his own friends and business taken away from him, but he didn't give up.

The idea of Mickey Mouse came after this. Disney's next venture, the fourth one, became the one we know today. He would go on to create an empire.

Heroes all have epic failure stories but persevere even when people stab them in the back or their businesses fail.

Disney's story had three drastically different types of failures, but each served as a lesson to him. His response was to learn from those failures and never let them hold him back from his dream.

Kevin Hart speaks of failing many times in comedy clubs, where audiences were silent or laughed at him, not at his jokes. But he kept going to comedy nights and performing.

Charlie Chaplin would continually sign up to act, even after a series of poor performances. The audience was throwing orange peels and coins at him on stage, but he persevered.

> *Failure is a learning curve for heroes, not a dead-end.*

WORKING ON FAILURE TO SUCCESS

Another hero with a similar story of failures is Milton Hershey.

His first failure was starting his own pop-up candy store, which failed because of the increasing price of sugar and his lack of knowledge in running a business.

His second failure was because he still didn't understand how to run a business—and the rent for the shop space cut out all his profits.

His third attempt, and probably the hardest moment of his life, was likely his last shot. His family had given up on him and told him to go out on his own. As he walked the streets, he had a clear idea that he wanted to work in caramel. He knew how to make amazing caramels and his past mistakes taught him all he needed to know.

He just needed to find a way to get the venture started.

Hershey got a touch of luck on this third attempt, which would never have happened if he hadn't made that third attempt.

"Luck is a dividend of sweat," Ray Kroc, founder of McDonald's, once said.

Heroes pursue their goal relentlessly and with that kind of persistence, luck eventually finds them.

When Hershey was walking those streets, figuring out how to get started again, he thought "It's all up to me now. I won't need much, just a small shed, a way to pay freight on my equipment, and a whole lot of work. I'm smarter now. I know I can earn a good living making caramels."

He was confident he could do it. He knew he could do it.

When his third venture was up and running, a man in a suit brought three pennies worth of caramels.

"Did you make this, young man?" the stranger asked.

Hershey smiled. "Yes, sir. They're my Crystal A's, the best caramels in America."

The suited stranger nodded. "I do believe they are! I wish they would keep fresh; I'd take some back to London with me."

Milton smiled, proud to tell the stranger that his caramels would last for months, a technique he learned from his second failure.

The stranger paused, and then after realizing how serious Hershey was, he pulled out his card and handed it to Milton. The card read: *Andrew Decies – Confectionary Importer.*

This importer gave him a large order; however, Milton needed more money to fulfill the order. Unfortunately, a person with two failed businesses and no assets was simply too great a risk. No bank was going to loan him the money he needed.

But, there happened to be one banker...

After Hershey was rejected from multiple banks, one particular banker, known to take risks, decided to take a chance and gave him a loan under the banker's name.

Hershey went to work, making the caramels every day, and then sent them off.

The week the loan was due, a letter arrived with five hundred pounds, enough to pay off his debts and pay for ingredients for another order of caramels. He rushed to the bank, exhilarated, and paid off the loan.

Over the next six years, Hershey would expand globally, filling orders from Australia, Japan, and China. He would generate millions of dollars of business a year and employ more than 800 people. Everyone knew about the caramels made by Hershey and his new company, the Lancaster Caramel Company.

FAILURE IS JUST A PROCESS

Some people fail multiple times, others may fail only once.

My own list of failures includes a handful of failed applications, seeming endless job rejections, and a whole list of rejected school applications. These didn't feel great, but in each failure I found something I could learn.

When my first mobile application failed, I realized that I didn't set a deadline—and so the app was never released. The next time I tried, I set a deadline. This app did get published, but with no marketing. So, I learned to prepare a marketing budget and plan for the third app.

It's a chain of lessons. If I didn't fail, I would never have known. When you're afraid of failing, you miss out on experiences, and more importantly, you won't know what works for *you* to achieve success.

Failure is part of the process. It's painful, but necessary.

Channel your heroes when you fail as often as that might be. When you fail an exam. When your company is about to go bankrupt. When you get fired from a job. Channel and ask yourself, What is the lesson? What can I do next time to get what I want?

You must persevere to get a result. You must stand back up after a failure.

Failure isn't the end. It's just a *part* of success. How many *times* you fail does not matter. *How* you fail does not matter. Backstabbing, poor timing, not knowing or being naive—these things happen, and you must take them as lessons and beneficial events that propel you forward to your goal.

> *If you don't realize that failure is a lesson, you cannot succeed. Because without defeat, there cannot be victory.*

5. TAKE OWNERSHIP OF YOUR LIFE

Taking ownership is extremely difficult, especially when you're at fault. If you can't admit your failures or your mistakes, how do you plan to take control of your life?

Taking ownership of everything you have done to this point is crucial for you to find *your* success. By owning up, you actually learn where to improve. You gain the respect of people around you.

I hate admitting to a mistake when I have done something wrong. Even when all the signs clearly indicate that it was my mistake, I try to convince myself that it can't be me.

When one of my companies decided to pivot into app development, I made a crucial mistake in assigning the wrong people to the task. It was really tempting for me to blame them. After all, they had agreed to the tasks that were assigned to them.

But when I finally got in front of the team, I couldn't help but realize it was my fault. I was the one who had assigned them.

I ended up beginning with "I'm sorry," and then went through my mistakes and why I should have involved everyone in the decisions. When I owned up to the mistake, something profound happened: Their perception of me changed. They started to talk to me more and suggested people for certain positions. They became more helpful and started taking responsibility for their own mistakes.

All of this helped me run the company.

When we decided to pivot again, we were able to succeed in developing a virtual reality game called Crazy Fishing VR.

You must take ownership even when it seems you will look bad. Owning up to your mistakes and errors will, in the long run, far outweigh any short-term gain.

OWNERSHIP COMMANDS RESPECT

Jocko Willink was a lieutenant commander in the Navy SEALS. Back when he was in Iraq, and in command of a large team, there was a problem. A mission was underway, but it went downhill.

It was not because of enemy fire, but because of friendly fire. It was known as a "blue on blue"—when someone from your own team shoots another team member. It was unheard of to have a blue on blue.

He already had to deal with the enemy, and now he had to worry about his own teammates? Jocko knew it wasn't looking good and word rapidly spread of the screw-up. People were disappointed. The list of mistakes was huge. When drawing up the timelines and maps, numerous people could be blamed, and everyone had contributed to one colossal failure.

But, in reality, there was only one person to blame…

Jocko knew who it was.

When Jocko had to report the mission, he stood up in front of his team and asked them one thing, "Whose mistake was it?"

Slowly, people started standing up and taking responsibility.

"It was my fault," one soldier said.

"It was because of me," said another.

But Jocko stopped them. Although there were many factors, he knew it all rested on him. He was responsible and he took complete ownership. Even if it meant getting fired, he told the team and the higher in command that it was ultimately his fault. They realized that he was someone willing to take the fall for the team. Someone willing to own up to their mistakes.

He didn't pass the blame and as a result he earned respect from his teammates, which would allow him to create successful teams in the Navy.

At all times you must take ownership and be willing to risk it all.

OWN YOUR DEFEAT, AND YOU WILL SUCCEED

Cassius Clay was a famous boxer who fought Sonny Liston. Even though Sonny "juiced" his gloves (a special liquid to blind his opponent), Clay—later known as Muhammad Ali—still won. The critical turning point in Ali's career was when he fought a man named Ken Norton.

Ali felt he was invincible. He thought this fight was going to be simple and expected to win. However, it was a grueling fight and in a split decision, Norton won. People were celebrating Ali's defeat.

Soon after the match, Ali was sent to the hospital—his jaw had been broken in one of the first few rounds.

In the hospital, Ali had time to think. "I didn't train right. I didn't rest. I played all night. Fighting is a serious, dangerous business, and I took it lightly…. This is the best thing that could've happened to me. I started believing that I couldn't be whipped. That I didn't have to work hard. That I didn't have to train hard."

Ali owned up to his mistakes.

He was ready to win.

When Ali realized it was his mistake, he took ownership of it. He had thrown himself into a lifestyle that didn't suit him. It was the reason he lost, and he knew it was his fault.

Ali trained for the next fourteen weeks at Deer Lake, the longest time he had ever spent training for a fight in his career. He became disciplined. Every morning at 4:30, he ran four miles and would chop down oak trees to build strength in his hands, arms and shoulders. In the gym, he continued to practice on both heavy bags and speed bags.

When he entered the ring again for a rematch with Norton, it was a close fight. It was only in the final rounds Ali was able to summon up strength for a flurry in the last seconds. Again, it was a split decision, but this time Ali was the winner.

His career was saved.

If Ali hadn't recognized his mistakes that caused him to lose the first match, his career would have ended. A second defeat to Norton would have written him off for good.

To improve and come back stronger, you must recognize when and what causes you to be defeated. What is in your control that you can change?

Take ownership of it. Change it.

BUILD SOLID FOUNDATIONS

Bob Iger, CEO of Disney, had a hero when he worked at ABC Sports named Roone Arledge. Arledge was meticulous.

When Frank Sinatra performed for ABC, Arledge wanted to re-do the entire show (even though Sinatra was to perform in a few hours). There was a deadline and it seemed impossible, but Arledge demanded the show be re-recorded. They set up a new stage with new angles for the cameras. And just before the deadline, the re-do was complete. That show became a massive success. But this perfectionism made it scary to disappoint Arledge.

One day, Iger was able to talk to Arledge.

"Some days, I have a tough time keeping my head above water," Iger told him.

Arledge quickly quipped, "Get a longer snorkel."

In other words: Work hard and adapt.

But Iger enjoyed working for Arledge. A pivotal point was when ABC was covering a lot of different sports. Iger was responsible for covering a new running world record in Norway. He didn't get the rights to air it and hoped no one would notice. However, during a team meeting, Arledge immediately asked the entire team: Who was responsible for this? Who failed to get the coverage? The room was silent.

Iger put his hand up, saying he was responsible, and it was his fault. Thirty heads turned to him. Silence again.

Then Arledge continued with the day's agenda.

After the meeting, people came up to Iger and told him they were shocked. "I can't believe you did that. No one ever does that, they said. How could he admit his mistake in front of Arledge? Wasn't he afraid of being fired?

But he wasn't afraid—or fired. From that day forward, Iger noticed that Arledge treated him with higher regard.

"In your work, in your life, you will be more respected and trusted by the people around you if you honestly own up to your mistakes," Iger wrote in his autobiography, *The Ride of a Lifetime.*

Lying and covering your own ass isn't going to work.

When you admit your mistakes, you create an environment that allows people to feel that they will be heard. It is OK to make honest mistakes. If you blame others or don't own your mistakes, it creates an environment of fear.

Iger notes that people feared Arledge because his perfection made people worried about upsetting him. This made them less willing to take risks or to try something new or innovative.

By taking ownership, you build a foundation that breeds honesty and trust. This will not only help you succeed, it will also help others around you as well.

When I make a mistake, I remember that mistakes are inevitable.

No hero was able to move forward without owning up to their mistakes. How would a golf pro know where to improve if he didn't admit his own failures? How can you grow if you think everything you do is someone else's mistake?

Steal from your heroes the willingness to own up to your own mistakes. You will better yourself and the people around you.

Take responsibility for the actions of those that you lead but also for your own actions with your team members. When one person wins, you all win.

"Implementing extreme ownership requires checking your ego and operating with a high degree of humility. Admitting mistakes, taking ownership, and developing a plan to overcome challenges are integral to any successful team," Jocko Willink said in his book, *Extreme Ownership.*

When I think of a moment to channel, I remember an advertisement from Domino's Pizza.

The CEO of Domino's, Patrick Doyle, stood up on national television and admitted to everyone that Domino's was crap. "Microwave pizza is far superior." He acknowledged the problems Domino's had, then reconfigured their core product and asked people to give them another try. Described as courageous, bold, and refreshing, it gave the company a positive light.

What happened in the end? Domino's sales rose, and profits nearly doubled in a single quarter.

Take ownership of your mistakes. Even when it's uncomfortable. Even when you might get fired. If you can take ownership of things in your life now, you can take control of what happens to you in your future.

6. PLAY WITH THE CARDS YOU ARE GIVEN

Sometimes I have compared myself to others. We all do this, as we emphasize the differences in our situation and decide to make ourselves feel worse off.

At times, it can be difficult *not* to compare.

I once met a guy who seemingly out of nowhere became rich. I complained that he didn't deserve it. But what did I know? How much work had he put in before his success? What trials and difficulties had he gone through?

I was poking a fire that was only burning me.

Comparing yourself to people who are in entirely different situations makes no sense. It doesn't help you.

You must work with what *you* have.

When something terrible happens to heroes, they don't sit still. They can be upset, but they move on as soon as possible.

Doyle Brunson lost his athletic abilities but became the godfather of poker. Helen Keller lost her vision and hearing, but still fulfilled her dream of graduating from college.

You may be tempted to stare at the cards you don't have like I did. Or complain about the cards that were apparently dealt to others. Or you may be angry because the deck was rigged.

Heroes don't have time for that.

They concentrate on the cards that are in their hands and play them the best they can.

NEVER STAY CRUSHED

A younger Doyle Brunson would be shocked if you had told him he was going to be a poker star. Raised on a cotton farm with no electricity or plumbing, Brunson would spend most of his time outdoors and training to become an athlete. At school, he would be selected for the state basketball team, the state track team, *and* the state baseball team.

The stars were aligning for Brunson.

"My future looked promising," Brunson says. "Like a boy's dream was going to come true."

Without a doubt, his dreams of being in the NBA were in reach, with the Lakers considering him as a possible first draft opportunity.

One fateful summer day though, when he was working in a gypsum plant, a forklift loading a big stack started to slip.

Overestimating his strength, Brunson ran forward and tried to hold the gypsum stack in place, but the two thousand pounds caught his leg and slid off. Before he knew it, his leg was mangled in all directions.

"It wasn't just my legs that got crushed," Brunson says, "it was my hopes, my dreams, everything I had been working for my entire younger life."

In his senior year of college, he hobbled around on crutches with no idea or direction on what to do.

Brunson would put his athletic dreams behind him. He decided to go to school to study executive education and business administration.

He kept moving. He was never sure if that was what he wanted—he just kept moving. He played with the cards he was dealt.

Eventually, he landed a job as a salesman. His second call was to a pool hall, where he stumbled on a poker game. He sat down and cleared a month's salary in less than three hours. He then wondered why he needed to work if he could make that kind of money playing poker?

He quit his job and began to concentrate on poker.

By the end of 1998, Doyle had won the World Championship of Poker twice, countless cash tournament games, and authored a globally recognized book on poker, *The Super System*.

"I can't tell you that the cards you're dealt will be the ones you want,"

Doyle says, "but whatever they turn out to be, play them wisely, and honestly, and with passion and pleasure. That's the secret."

The secret to Brunson's success is that he kept moving. When he no longer could be an athlete, he kept figuring out what he *could* do. He could have stayed upset about his broken leg and his shattered dreams. But he didn't. He played the cards he was given. He didn't mope around. His sports dreams were behind him, so he searched for another route to success.

And that happened to be playing cards.

SHE WAS BORN WITH IT

Helen Keller would lose her vision and hearing at a very young age. She was initially upset, but with the assistance of her teacher, she didn't give up hope. She learned words by using her hands and sense of touch. The teacher would spell in her hand the letters d-o-l-l, and then give her a doll to hold and feel. There were tough moments.

"But I kept on trying," Keller says, "knowing that patience and perseverance would win in the end."

Keller was literally limited in what she could do. She was overwhelmed initially but got over the hurdle. She accepted her situation. She then pursued and succeeded in attending and graduating college—her lifelong dream.

Keller wrote in her autobiography, *The Story of My Life*, "When one door of happiness closes, another opens; but often we look so long at the closed door that we do not see the one which has been opened for us."

Bill Klein and Dr. Jen Arnold are two people born with skeletal dysplasia. Even when people would insult them and call them "midgets" they didn't let it affect them.

Jen was judged for her pursuits in the medical field because she was short.

Bill heard comments made about his height, and people laughed and pointed at him during his job hunt in New York. Bill was rejected countless times while looking for a job in sales. One even denied him a job because they told him he was invisible.

"My height never held me back," Bill says. "The beauty of not being handed everything is you appreciate what you have and enjoy working on what you want."

They accepted the cards they were given and started to support each other, creating a successful TV show called *The Little People*.

These heroes concentrated on what they *could* do.

Although they were born with conditions that didn't favor them, they chose to play the cards they were dealt. You can't change what you have, but you can certainly change your perspective. They didn't complain or reject who they were.

Reality can be painful, but concentrating on the negatives or the constraints can genuinely prevent you from achieving your goals.

CONSTRAINTS ARE GOOD

We often think that constraints are bad. But when you look at them closely, amazing things have come from constraints.

Look at how *The Cat in the Hat* was made.

Life magazine had reported that children were not learning to read because their books were boring, and television was competing for their attention.

Consequently, William Spaulding, a director of an educational publishing company, challenged Theodor Seuss Geisel—later known to the world as Dr. Seuss—to write a book that first graders would not want to put down, but also would have no more than 225 unique words selected from a list of 348.

Within three years, the resulting book would sell near a million copies with numerous translations.

Then in 1960, Bennett Cerf, another director, bet Dr. Seuss could not write a book with exactly fifty unique words. Dr. Seuss turned these extreme limitations into a work of art, creating *Green Eggs and Ham*, which would be his best seller, with almost 200 million copies sold worldwide.

Look at the cards or limitations you are given. Instead of being upset about them or worrying, figure out how you can play them best.

Some of your best works will come from your own constraints.

I remember walking with a friend of mine in Canada. She wasn't born rich. In fact, she lived on food stamps throughout her childhood.

But if you looked at her now, you would have never guessed it.

She runs a very successful real estate company and when I found out about her past, I asked what it was like growing up. I came to realize that her success began when she accepted her family wasn't wealthy. She began to work part-time jobs. She worked as much as she could to afford to take herself through university.

In doing this, she was able to change her circumstances. She learned business on her own. She hustled to find her first house to sell by knocking on the doors of her neighbors.

She doesn't know that I call her a hero, but she sure is one to me.

What we must steal from these heroes is their acceptance. These heroes accept the cards they are given. They concentrate on what they can do. From that acceptance, they can achieve the things they set out to do.

If they can't find a path that suits them, they search for another. They don't concentrate on options that are no longer available to them. If they can't find a satisfactory solution, then they create one that works for them.

Acceptance minimizes downtime while maximizing your time in achieving what you want.

Some people will be dealt good cards. Others will be dealt even better ones. You have no time to worry about what *they* have. You only have time to worry about what *you* can do.

Work with what you have. Make the best moves with the cards you are dealt.

When you find yourself complaining about something that has already been dealt to you, channel these heroes.

When you find yourself asking why you have it worse off than others, channel these heroes.

Remind yourself that they were able to succeed by playing with what they had, even though their decks seemed rigged against them. They accepted and persevered.

As Doyle Brunson can attest to in many of his poker games:

The best hand doesn't always win. It's how you play the hand you're dealt that matters.

7. CHANGE COMES FROM WITHIN

Change must come from within. As much as you may want to quit smoking or gambling or lose weight, if you don't want your goal enough, you won't obtain it. Many heroes must face their demons to succeed. Many heroes had to change their internal beliefs before they could achieve their goals.

HEROES HAVE VICES

Heroes are human and, like you and me, they have vices. Things that suppress or hold them back from achieving either their potential or their goals.

Nikola Tesla got over his gambling addiction with the help of his mother. Knowing that he loved playing cards, she decided to give him the family savings. After seeing how upset his mum was, Tesla decided he had to quit. He conquered his addiction instantly.

Jay-Z had decided that his life would be stuck in hustling the streets, selling drugs, but he came to the realization that he could do way better—and he did. He wanted to own a record company, and that's precisely what he set out to do.

Jon Hamm, famous for playing Don Draper in *Mad Men,* decided he needed a change after being rejected on *The Bachelorette*. Hamm chose to become the "sexiest man alive" and seemingly out of nowhere he achieved just that (he was voted as *People*'s "Sexiest Man Alive" in 2010).

These individuals *wanted* change in their lives—and it happened.

A close friend of mine was addicted to smoking. I told him of all the problems of smoking: the expense of it, how he reeked of tobacco, and how it could destroy his health. He was aware of all of this, but he just couldn't quit.

A year later, I had noticed he was no longer smoking. I asked him what he did, and he simply said, "I just wanted to quit."

You can't convince people to improve their lives, even if you have all the studies to support your claims, or even if it's just pure common sense. *They need to want to make the necessary changes.*

For us to be like our heroes, we must want the change.

BEING TOLD YOU HAVE NO FUTURE

Marilyn Monroe was told time and time again to give up her dreams of being an actor because she had no talent.

"I knew how third rate I was," Marilyn reflected. "I could actually feel my lack of talent.

The producers didn't help. They told her that she was ugly. When she performed in actual movie parts, the editors would purposely cut her face out so she would never be shown on camera.

Her dreams were walking out the door.

But she had a change of heart. She decided that she could play any part if she worked hard for it.

Marilyn invested her money on drama, dancing, and singing lessons. She kept improving. There were times she would sneak away with movie scripts and, all alone, would read them aloud in front of the mirror.

"I fell in love with myself, not who I was but who I was going to be," she wrote in her biography, *My Story*.

Marilyn concentrated on the only factors she could change, and that all started from within. It was as if her attitude flipped. No one made that decision for her; she made it on her own. The world seemed to respond in kind. She would star in a few small movies that would turn her life around.

"When you have only a single dream, it is more than likely to come true—because you keep working toward it without getting mixed up."

WHAT YOU BELIEVE, YOU WILL BECOME

Your beliefs can hold you back. If you believe you can't do something, you won't. You can convince yourself to fail. Or perhaps even unknowingly sabotage yourself.

One time I had an interview for a job and felt like I was going to fail regardless. Consequently, for weeks I decided to play computer games and no longer practice. I believed so strongly that there was no point to revise or study for the interview that I made failure the only result.

When I did have the interview, I was asked questions that I could have easily practiced and answered. I left the interview upset with myself. I fulfilled my own prophecy. Had I believed I even had a shot at succeeding, I could have gotten the job.

But I didn't.

What you believe is very important. Change comes from within. You must, without any doubt, think that you can do what you set out to do.

If I told you that a famous surgeon was known to have a bad temper and had stabbed a friend with a knife, you would be pretty concerned. Ben Carson was just that doctor.

When he was young, his temper was uncontrollable. Carson had hit his mother. He once attempted to stab a friend; fortunately, his friend's belt buckle deflected the knife.

"If people could make me angry, they could control me. Why should I give someone else such power over my life?" Carson reflected.

Although he wanted to be a doctor, Carson knew that if he had a temper, he could never achieve such a goal.

After almost stabbing his friend, Carson had run into the bathroom to hide, ashamed of what he had done. Wiping away tears, Carson made a vow. He was going to get rid of his anger and control his temper. Reflecting on all his other horrible moments, he realized that he was responsible.

He changed right then and there.

Overnight, he became a new person. He picked himself up and joined the Reserve Officer Training Corps.

After that, with only enough money to enter college to study medicine, he applied to Yale and was accepted.

"Whatever direction we choose," Carson said, "if we can realize that every hurdle we jump strengthens and prepares us for the next one, we're already on the way to success."

Dr. Carson would eventually be the first surgeon to perform a successful hemispherectomy on a child (literally removing half the patient's brain). It was a breakthrough event.

Who would have thought that a person who almost stabbed his friend would use the knife for good?

I HATE THIS SUIT

No person or coach alone can change you. No book can change you. You must want it *first*, and then seek the necessary things to create that change.

In 2012, Felix Baumgartner jumped from a helium balloon in the stratosphere and landed in New Mexico. In doing so, he set the world record for skydiving, reaching a top speed of 843 mph.

But Felix had not always been set on skydiving.

In fact, he had to see a psychologist to fight his fear, a fear he had never encountered before.

When he first wore a jumpsuit designed for lengthy skydives, he felt unwell. Was it the fear of the jump? Or the fear of falling? The answer was the suit itself. Consequently, he stopped jumping.

Since he was not making any progress, another skydiver replaced him.

The moment Felix saw the replacement diver wearing the suit, he became upset. It struck a nerve. He would have to do something about his fear.

"This is my suit," he said to himself. But for him to wear it, he needed to change.

Surprisingly, Felix was scared of the suit because he was used to freedom. To him, being locked up in a restrictive suit was no laughing matter. The only way he could get past this barrier was to find a solution that would work for him.

He knew he was preventing himself from jumping, so he began scuba diving and working on his mental skills.

Felix then wore the suit until he had a panic attack, and then would do simple math calculations or spell words backward to keep his mind off his fears.

It worked. Felix would go on to complete a record-breaking leap and conquered his fears completely.

So, when you want to change, you must make sure the first person who wants that change is *you*.

People can tell you what they think, and perhaps guide you in the right direction, but if *you* don't want it, if *you* don't care, it just won't happen.

Even as I write this chapter, I am reminded of telling myself that I would eat healthily every day. Yet for years I would buy unhealthy food and just eat junk food whenever I could.

I didn't really want it. My skin was breaking out. I was out of shape. Friends told me to work on my diet. Personal training friends tried to convince me.

Nothing happened.

Then one day, I realized I should just do it. When I saw myself in the mirror, I wanted the change more than anything else. I took everything out of the fridge and pantry. I was going to eat healthily and haven't looked back.

Heroes had weaknesses they had to overcome. They were told they were useless or that they couldn't do something. From within, heroes decided that they could change. No matter what the world said, they knew they could do it.

Steal from them the belief that you are capable of change.

Once you believe in something, start making the necessary moves to ensure it happens. Believe you can build a business? Then go ahead and do it. Want to quit an addiction? Done. You have decided it, and you will get there.

Whatever the goal, whatever the change, it's possible—and it starts with you.

8. SURROUND YOURSELF WITH RIGHT PEOPLE

Heroes tend to surround themselves with the *right* people. Surround yourself with people who will support and push you to achieve what you want.

Michael Dell would never have considered making full-fledged computers and never would have founded Dell Computers without the help of a visiting customer.

J.R.R. Tolkien would never have published *The Hobbit*. It wasn't until someone heard of an unfinished, but remarkable, children's story Tolkien had written, and then convinced him that it was worth publishing.

Similarly, Stephen King was able to produce his first big novel because his wife found and pulled out his manuscript in the bin.

THEY NUDGE YOU ALONG

King had almost given up on writing. He had found an English teaching job in the nearby town of Hampden. He was barely making a living and lived in a doublewide trailer.

"If I ever came close to despairing about my future as a writer, it was then," King said.

To make enough money, he would clean bathrooms, and oddly enough, that was where he got the idea for a story about a girl with supernatural abilities. He went home and wrote the first few pages. He felt he was onto something.

But then, something came over him, and he thought it didn't click. He threw the draft away and that was going to be the end of it.

Perhaps it was a twist of fate that his wife, Tabby, decided to clean his study that day. She went through the rubbish and found a manuscript with cigarette ashes all over the pages. She smoothed out and read them, loving what she saw. When King arrived home, she told him to keep writing it.

"Having someone who believes in you makes a lot of difference. They don't have to make speeches. Just believing is usually enough," King reflected.

Carrie would be his first published novel, and it was a huge hit. He ended up with $200,000 in the bank, and the beginning of a prolific writing career.

Without his wife's support, he might still be in the trailer park, teaching English, and cleaning bathrooms. Tabby supported and encouraged him to follow his passion. She helped set up a makeshift desk for him in the laundry room. While King wrote, she would help look after their newborn toddler.

To understand how much she supported his goals, when King found another way to make extra income, she asked, "Will you have time to write?"

He responded, "Not much."

What did Tabby say? "Then you can't take the job."

The right people will push you toward achieving your goals. Not all heroes can do it alone. Somewhere along the way, the people they surround themselves with continually nudge them in the right directions, reminding them of what they were pursuing.

Support is hard to find, but genuine support may be the reason you will find success.

Be selective with whom you hang around and share your goals. They will be the people who will want your success no matter what.

YOU CAN LEARN FROM THE PEOPLE AROUND YOU

Working with a single person as a sole guide isn't always the best way we learn new things. Sometimes we need more than one person to influence or support us.

Jack Ma, the founder of Alibaba, learned English by doing just that. Every morning before dawn, he would ride to a hotel and provide *free* tours to tourists visiting China. In doing so, he would learn English from them. He gave his free tours for more than nine years and today is fluent in English.

During his free tours, Jack met a man named Ken Morley. Perhaps as a testament to his networking ability, or the fact he met so many people during these free tours, they formed a friendship and became pen pals. Ken took Jack under his wing and helped subsidize his studies at college. Jack Ma has since attributed many of his successes to this friendship.

Kerry Stokes, chairman of Seven Network, one of Australia's largest broadcast corporations, also surrounded himself with people he could learn from. When he was trying to improve his English, he hired an Englishman as his employee. Stokes was able to learn vocabulary and manners that helped him create a media empire.

Surrounding yourself with people who are better than you is certainly not a new concept.

"One of the best things you can do in life is to surround yourself with people who are better than you are: high-grade people," Warren Buffett once said. Buffett was secretly afraid of public speaking. To address this, he would surround himself with people who suffered the same fear. They learned from each other and conquered that fear together. Today, watching any of his shareholder meetings at Berkshire, you would have no clue he ever feared public speaking.

Who you choose to associate yourself with matters.

Surrounding yourself with people you can learn from will continually encourage you to keep improving.

So surround yourself with confident people in the areas you want to improve. Learn and steal from them. Absorb.

AVOID THE WRONG PEOPLE

But what happens if you form friendships with the wrong people?

Some people will try to pull you down. The more you surround yourself with such people, the lower you will pull *yourself* down.

Arnold Schwarzenegger wanted to compete for Mr. Universe in London. Having partied hard and with his ambition beginning to slip, he again focused on his training. The goal was no longer to have fun but to become a world champion bodybuilder.

He had sent his application to participate in the competition way ahead of time but hadn't heard back in weeks.

With a few weeks left before the deadline for applications, he decided to contact London and found out they had never received his application. Frantically trying to find out why, Schwarzenegger found out that his own boss and trainer, Rolf Putziger, had found his application in the outgoing mail and threw it away. Putziger was jealous. He didn't want Schwarzenegger to succeed, but instead wanted to make as much money off Schwarzenegger as possible. He would do anything in his power to prevent Schwarzenegger from leaving. He was trying to cage the bird.

It was fortunate that Schwarzenegger would end up in a good relationship with another trainer, Albert. Albert called London and tried to persuade the Mr. Universe organizers to let Schwarzenegger in. Luckily, they agreed even though the deadline had passed, and they put him on the list.

Chosen as runner-up, a massive victory for him at the time, Schwarzenegger built a mindset that allowed him to repeatedly win. "After that," he said, "I never went to a competition to compete. I went to win."

As you will find out later, it was this drive and vision that allowed Schwarzenegger to succeed in many fields of his life.

And what happened to Putziger? He would have succeeded if he had simply supported Schwarzenegger in his ambitions and goals. Having a bodybuilding champion come out of your gym would be beneficial for both the gym and the trainer. But Putziger wasn't supportive and lost all the advantages of ever having been a part of Schwarzenegger's eventual legacy.

If you surround yourself with the wrong people, you might prevent your own success from happening, which means you might not achieve your goals. The time that heroes allocate to others is finite. They choose very carefully who they surround themselves with and when they realize someone is toxic to them, they get up and leave.

Knowing when to leave isn't always easy but when you see the red flags, make your move as soon as possible. You don't have time for toxic people who distract you from your goals.

So, surround yourself with the right people whether they are mentors or those who share similar goals. You need these supportive people in your life.

Give yourself time to take stock of the people around you. Are they bringing you down? Are they preventing you from achieving what you want? You don't need to burn bridges with these relationships, but you certainly can spend less time maintaining them.

Heroes know they can only spend so much of their time and mental space with certain people. So, they make sure these people count. Steal their ability to be with the people that will help you succeed in life. You're not judging people. You're being honest with yourself.

Be with people who support your goals and dreams.

There was a time I was calculating in my friendships. I wanted to surround myself with people who would benefit me. I would just take from them. No giving. Just taking.

The problem was that my relationships couldn't survive in that kind of imbalance.

People figure you out.

Whenever I met someone, I would run a system in my head, and if the person didn't benefit me, I wouldn't give them much time.

This was stupid.

Now, when I meet someone, I'm reminded that heroes don't calculate. They invest deeply in rewarding relationships. They eventually weed out the people who prevent them from achieving their goals.

But you see, when you meet someone, you honestly never know. You must give a person a chance because that person might turn out to be pivotal in your life. Perhaps they could be a hero who will help you to achieve your goals. If not, you simply move on and keep surrounding yourself with amazing people.

Forget the rest.

9. ALWAYS LEARN

There is one constant in *your* journey—and that is *you*. You must work on yourself because that is the one thing you can improve every day. Heroes are continually learning and working on themselves. Even if they are known as the best in their field, they continue learning and growing.

Warren Buffett created a habit of always reading and learning new things, saying, "That's how knowledge builds up … like compound interest."

Jack Ma woke up every day to learn English and improve his social skills before he founded Alibaba.

Benjamin Franklin continually worked on himself with visits to a library, where he spent a few hours a day in "constant study."

Always work on yourself. Continuously learn and improve, so you aren't left behind.

BE DELIBERATE IN YOUR LEARNING

I have made the mistake of studying something just for the sake of studying. I learned to program but had no clue what it was for.

Once I had an idea of *why* I needed to learn something, I became more comfortable with it and learned it a lot faster.

At the time, I wanted to make a simple iPhone game.

I took up the programming language known as C#. By using tutorials and guides, I was able to make the game, *Scramble 7*. It didn't make any money, but I did finish it.

Having a clear idea of *why* and *what* I wanted to make improved my learning.

You can get stuck in a cycle of aimless learning, tricking yourself into thinking you're making progress. But, in reality, you're unsure what to do, so whatever it may be, you aren't actually getting anywhere with it. You must be deliberate.

Directed study is working toward a defined goal.

That means that what you're studying has a purpose and moves you closer to your goal. This is what sets your heroes apart. There's a *reason* they are learning what they are learning.

Derek Sivers, a musician, was able to learn to code because he had a clear idea of creating an online platform for musicians to distribute their CDs. Milton Hershey learned more about chocolate once he realized that chocolate was the next "big hit."

These heroes directed their study.

Anders Ericsson's study on deliberate practice famously demonstrates that you must be intentional in your practice. That is, you are continually working to your upper limits and doing harder problems. By doing so, you will be able to master and learn much faster (like playing a difficult piano piece vs. playing an easy one).

Heroes will always be deliberate once they set a goal. They know where they are headed and they will make sure to learn everything they can to get there.

LEARN TO SUCCEED

Soichiro Honda, before founding the Honda Company, was a mechanic who kept learning. During his journey, he tried to make car pistons. But when Honda's first batch of car pistons failed (94% of them), he realized he didn't know enough.

"Success," Honda said, "can be achieved only through repeated failure and introspection. In fact, success represents one percent of your work, which results only from the ninety-nine percent that is failure."

So, what did he do when he failed?

He immediately realized his lack of knowledge and directed his study. He needed to know more about metallurgy, so he enrolled in the Hamamatsu School of Technology, where he learned with determined focus on steelmaking, machine techniques, stamping, tool-making dies, and manufacturing designs.

He would immediately drop out once he felt he had enough knowledge.

"What I want is knowledge," Honda said when he reflected about studying.

He then created Tokai Seiki Heavy Industry and ended up holding 28 patents related to piston rings and manufacturing.

For Honda to succeed, he had to learn more. He realized he lacked the knowledge and threw himself into improving his weakness.

Warren Buffett always planned to have a career in investing. Although he had already started a successful business by setting up a paper route and earning a full-time wage managing the company, he began to study stock tables.

He studied so much that word of his knowledge had followed him to school, where his teachers would even ask him about the market.

Not only did he analyze stocks, but he also worked on improving his public speaking. He taught a night class at the University of Omaha where, because of his young age, doctors and older students snickered at the young Buffett teaching them investing techniques. Buffett was doing double-duty learning by working on his fear of public speaking while diving into investing.

But to really further his knowledge, he needed to learn from other people. And he had heroes. He studied their successes by learning from Rose Blumkin, who built a large furniture business in Omaha on only $500.

He also deepened his knowledge by studying under Benjamin Graham, an economist and legendary investor, who eventually became Buffett's mentor.

It was through these people that he would learn the fundamentals of value investing. According to Buffett, this changed his life and set him on the path of investing.

The renowned basketball Hall of Famer, Michael Jordan, had to restart multiple times in his career. When he played in a state tournament, he got fouled off and ended his high school basketball career in disappointment. It had mattered a lot to him and he decided to train again. He believed he had excellent skills, but Jordan knew he had to keep learning.

"My greatest skill was being teachable," Jordan observed. "I was like a sponge."

These heroes find what they need to achieve their goals and learn it. And then, they keep learning, even when they are at their seeming pinnacle, they strive for more.

TIME IS FINITE

To succeed you must be deliberate in your learning and always work on improving yourself.

Marc Cuban wrote in his book, *How to Win*, "I may be sitting in front of the TV, but I'm not watching it, unless I think there is something I can learn from it."

That's not to say you shouldn't have a break, but it's as if every hero concentrates on their goal so much it becomes an obsession. They *want* to learn more. They *want* to maximize their time.

For Andre Agassi to move back up in the tennis rankings when he was at his lowest, he would train and work on his skills every day.

For Gordon Ramsay, it was to cook under a tyrant and learn more techniques.

You must always want to learn. To do this takes time, and time is a finite resource. Use it well and use it efficiently.

Benjamin Franklin is famous for his five-hour rule. He was an author, inventor, and entrepreneur. He also left school when he was ten.

In fact, many heroes left school early: Bill Gates, Henry Ford, and John D. Rockefeller to name a few.

This five-hour rule was not five hours a day, but five hours every week devoted to learning. It doesn't mean you should give yourself five hours *only*, but you can learn a lot if you lock in and dedicate five hours to learning a week. We can't let anything impede our learning process.

I am guilty of having distractions all around me. When I first started studying by myself, I would have my mobile phone next to me. It pinged, vibrated, and distracted me. If it wasn't my phone, it was a Web page I had opened.

I don't have the self-control yet that those heroes have, so I have learned to put these distractions away when I'm learning something new. Whether playing guitar, learning a language, or studying code, I dedicate a specific time and focus on that single task.

Steal from these heroes the desire to learn. You must always want to learn. Don't give it minimal effort or you might as well not be learning.

You must learn with clear intent.

If you want to master cooking, don't just learn the recipes you know but the ones you *wish* you knew. If you want to learn how to code, then learn how to program projects that you would almost have no clue how to tackle.

In their time, many heroes had to learn through books and papers. We have the advantage of learning online for free. You don't need to go to school if you have a clear direction on where you want to head. Find what you need to know. Write it down and tackle each subject, one by one.

> *Learning is an essential component to success, and every single hero does it, whether it be sports, business, or entertainment. Keep learning.*

Channel the moments when you get distracted. The moments that you realize that you aren't learning or challenging yourself. These heroes dedicated themselves as if it were the only thing they had to do. They worked on their craft and kept learning.

Remind yourself that you have time and a reason to study. You are working on a single constant in your life—*you*.

10. DON'T QUIT YOUR DAY JOB

We have been told time and time again that to succeed, you must throw yourself 100% into something. Quit your day job. Dedicate all your time to the one thing.

There have been heroes who *do* throw themselves 100% into something, but it's generally the case that they do this because they can afford to do so.

Mozart, for example, trained while very young and his father provided for him until he could succeed. Charles Darwin, who was born into both class and wealth, enjoyed luxury while working on his theory of evolution.

We want to believe that heroes throw away everything to pursue their goals, and perhaps there are a few exceptions. However, the majority are methodical and plan out how they can throw themselves into working on their dreams.

Contrary to popular belief, heroes make sure they have a plan first.

HEROES DON'T QUIT. WHY SHOULD YOU?

I was brought up believing that the great leaders of today discarded everything to pursue their dreams. It's a fantastic story, after all.

Paul Mitchell, founder of John Paul Mitchell Systems (a very successful shampoo company), started with only a few hundred dollars in his pocket. To get the company going, he would shower at the Griffith Park Tennis courts and eat eggs on toast for less than a dollar to save money. He also slept in his car and bargain hunted endlessly. Each dollar saved meant an extra dollar for his company.

Stories like this fuel us with the belief that you should go "all in." But most heroes don't. The reality is they give everything they possibly can with what they have. They only quit their day jobs when it is possible.

If you have the means to do so, quit your job. Dedicate all your time and effort to your goal. But there is certainly nothing wrong with keeping your day job to survive.

Jeff Bezos threw himself into Amazon *after* securing enough funding to dedicate himself to growing the company. In other words, he made sure he could survive and spend all his time on the company first, *then* did it. Netflix could only be created once it effectively secured around $2 million in funding.

We have romanticized that you should almost live in a car and eat only ramen noodles while funneling all your resources into your project or passion. You should do that so long as you can afford to and with consideration to people who are dependent on you. You can't do that if you have a wife or a husband or kids.

Dale Carnegie, the author of the bestseller, *How to Win Friends and Influence People*, wrote his book when he lived in a dingy apartment and in poverty. When he described his tiny apartment, he says, "I had a bunch of neckties hanging on the walls, and when I reached out to get a fresh necktie, the roaches scattered in all directions."

In doing so, he was able to concentrate on teaching to make money and writing a bestseller, which continues to sell to this day. He chose a lifestyle that suited his goals.

LIVING AT BARE MINIMUM

It could make sense to go bare minimum, depending on your goal.

Andrew Hallam, the author of *Millionaire Teacher,* ate meat from shells on the beach and showered in public change rooms so he could save as much money as possible and invest in index funds.

Walt Disney chose to write comics and live in absolute poverty alone—

one shower a week and canned beans for food—so he could pursue his dream of drawing.

Judy Wicks opened the Free People's Store only because she decided to live in the store itself. The store sold vintage clothing and she was so meticulous in caring for all her merchandise that she ran a customer down for stealing a pair of jeans.

It is at this level you can achieve your *greatest* potential. In order to really find your upper limit, you must remove all the unnecessary things from your life that are consuming your time and resources. Then you can direct everything you have toward your goals and dreams. Wouldn't you want to find what your top limit is?

But this doesn't mean you should just quit your day job; you still need to live.

Venture capitalist, Ben Horowitz, in his bestselling book, *The Hard Thing About Hard Things,* says that you should stabilize yourself first before quitting your job.

"I stopped thinking about myself and focused on what was best for my family. I started being the person that I wanted to be."

You certainly can't control your future if you can't control your current situation.

Get everything in order first, then start trimming.

The Wright Brothers, who created one of the very first man-made flight planes, didn't quit their day jobs in pursuit of their dream. When they worked on a flying contraption, they did it in their spare time. To survive, they began selling and repairing bicycles to fund their flying contraptions. It may seem as if they didn't go "all in," but they did. Every moment outside their job was spent trying to make an "aeroplane" so humans could fly.

Stephen King managed a teaching job and a cleaning job while writing his first best-selling book.

Einstein still had a job at the patent office, examining different patent applications (he arrived at work at 8 A.M. every day, six days a week). Yet during that time, he managed to produce a torrent of papers (sixteen from 1906 to 1907).

HEROES PLAN TO QUIT

So, when do heroes quit their day jobs? When they can afford to do so. You don't carelessly leave everything to pursue what you want. Contrary to popular belief, you do need to have a plan.

Sal Khan, founder of Khan Academy, was still working in finance when his idea of Khan Academy came to mind. He was teaching students mathematics and started making YouTube videos to teach them. He was enjoying it, so he made his own website and it grew. More viewers and more students. Although he could see a trend, did he quit his job then? He did not.

Even when he was asked to concentrate all his efforts into building Khan Academy, he said, "The thought of giving up a regular paycheck was scary ... neither of us was eager to revisit the financial austerity of our childhoods. So, I was still wavering."

He had a new child and a house; he couldn't just put all his resources into his project. But he planned. He made the jump to quit his job when he had enough savings to last him for nine months or so. From there, through a bit of luck, Khan Academy started receiving large grants from Google and the Bill and Melinda Gates Foundation. Today, Khan Academy continues to grow and teach everyone around the world, myself included.

Sam Walton, before founding Walmart, needed a plan before he committed himself to buying a convenience store. He would save $5000 to buy the shop and borrow $20,0000 to keep it running.

Even Nike founder, Phil Knight, created a clear plan before he decided to jump into selling sneakers. When he first went to Japan and ordered a few pair of sneakers, he felt he was onto a winner, but did he quit his job? Nope. Knight was still working at an accounting firm. He sent the new shoes to his track coach and they eventually became partners. To get the sale of the sneakers going, he would sell them out of a van and hustle as much as he could. He went to track meets and connected with runners and fans. Sales started to climb.

At that point, he finally decided to quit his job and begin his new shoe company.

DO SOMETHING ON THE SIDE

It is seen as a romanticized ideal that we should make money from what we love. If we don't, we apparently aren't doing it right. Why not make money and still do what you love on the side?

It was not like Steve jobs wanted to create Apple. Starting out, he dropped out of college, but remained on campus to clean floors and eat free meals. He then went to work at Atari and had another spiritual trip through India. Was this the story of a man who would end up creating one the most significant technology companies?

When he returned, he didn't quit his job, but he did notice something: People were falling in love with model-kit computers. He set up a plan to sell these kits with his friend, Steve Wozniak.

Did either of them quit their jobs? Not at all.

To them, this was a side project. They never expected it would grow into a large company.

The story, however, does become a legend soon after. Steve would go into a computer store, barefoot, and offer these kits for sale. The owner, Terrell, would give him a new idea to sell these kits pre-made. Jobs jumped at the concept and the rest is history.

Our day jobs can get boring. I'm reminded of that every day I go to work. I have always thought about and daydreamed of what it would be like to quit and do what I love.

But I realize that we can fall prey to dreaming and never end up doing anything.

When I started to work on side projects, my day job became enjoyable because I now saw it as something that allowed me to continue building what I wanted. My day job gave me the time to work on what I loved. Like these heroes, I need to plan a temporary exit. That way, I can live to my comfortable bare minimum while driving myself 100% into my project. Only then will I know if it will succeed.

Steal from heroes the patience to continue your day job until you can plan your next move.

Heroes don't just quit their day job, they plan. They experiment while they are still working. The difference is that once they feel a little catch and start to realize they have something—they form a plan to make it work. They find a way to make sure they can afford to quit their job by finding resources (from family, friends, or shareholders). Then, by living at a bare minimum, and by making sure they put in 100% of the effort, they concentrate on their goals and dreams.

So, while you're working on your own goals, work on them every hour you possibly can. You have made a bet and you need to see it to the end. Maximize your resources. Don't quit your day job just yet, but once you feel a bite on your line, don't hesitate to make a plan to devote yourself to your pursuit.

11. FOLLOW YOUR INCLINATIONS

The thought of following your passion sounds amazing, but do heroes follow their passion? *Sometimes.* Should you? *It really depends.*

Heroes follow their passion if it happens to align with what they are good at it *or* they have the luxury to pursue it. If you have all the resources you need, then of course you can follow your passions. But how many of us live in that kind of situation?

When I saw a friend running a little coffee shop, I asked him how he got started. He was a coffee lover, so I thought his passion got him there. He told me his parents gave him the money to try out his business venture.

At first I felt jealous but then realized that if I was in that situation, I would do the same. If you had access to resources to pursue what you want, you would use them.

His coffee shop has since done well and he's enjoying every bit of it. He got to do his passion and make a living from it.

Some heroes do what they are good at first—and then pursue their passions after.

Andre Agassi, although reaching number one in tennis, actually hated tennis (but he was damn good at it, obviously!).

> *There is nothing wrong with passion, but you need to know how and when you should pursue it.*

There are many heroes who succeeded in making their passions their job. J.K. Rowling was told she shouldn't write. Kevin Hart was told not to do comedy. Marilyn Monroe was advised not to act.

But they were successful. Why? Because they dedicated themselves to making themselves good at their passions.

If these heroes prove anything, it is that you can be good at something so long as you dedicate the time and genuine effort to perfect it. However, not all of us have the luxury to become a master. These heroes scraped by with a dedication to becoming good at their passion.

J.K Rowling was in poverty with a child. Kevin Hart and Marilyn Monroe were barely surviving. But they still had the means to live. They still needed to look after themselves.

As discussed in the previous chapter about living at a bare minimum—if you can afford to do so, do it—the world never said no to the passion of those who could do so. They were merely willing to pursue it relentlessly.

THE 10,000 HOURS MYTH

The 10,000-hour rule has been discussed endlessly...

You need 10,000 hours to become the master of a thing.

The core of this principle is straightforward: Genetics, age, when you start, and how you practice *all* affect how long it will take for you to become a master. There is no precise amount of time: It just naturally takes a damn long time.

Of course, Mozart perfected composing musical scores at the age of three! Of course, Usain Bolt can run really fast and has acknowledged that his genetics helped him. "My raw talent was out of this world. I used to cruise through practice and get by," he said.

Heroes realize their inclinations and dive deeper into them. It would make sense to take the fastest route possible.

If you require the least amount of time to master something, get there first, then learn something new after.

Everyone has an inclination. It will take time, but intuitively you will find it.

My friend, who has a ridiculous talent for graphic design, told me every day that his job was tedious and that he wanted to quit. He felt he needed to do something else but couldn't figure out what. He was getting paid exceptionally well, and work that took others days to accomplish only took him hours.

When he asked me for some suggestions, I told him to stay with his job because it has benefits he overlooked. It allowed him to venture into new fields. Why be upset with the hand that feeds you?

Be good at your inclinations. You won't need the 10,000 hours.

Felix Dennis wrote, "Your inclinations do really count. You have to pay attention to them." Although Felix loved art and poetry, he knew that he didn't possess the natural affinity for them. Still, after delving into his inclination, he was later able to afford that luxury.

He first tried singing and persuaded a few musicians to listen to him as he sang R&B (those musicians were John Lennon and Yoko Ono). What happened? He was told he was no good and that he had no real "voice." He argued. He left angry and still pushed to sing, even after he was told it wouldn't work.

He did eventually quit because he found his aptitude in selling.

He started with a magazine series made of eight-page, full-color, folded posters and simply sold them as poster magazines, which became a huge hit. It would be the start of his publishing company, which soon published hit magazines such as *Maxim*. He found his inclination and went with it.

DESTINED TO BE A SHOWMAN

There was a man who worked as a storekeeper, eventually opening a general store that sold bits and pieces. People loved him, and it was a successful store. That man, P.T. Barnum, would not be remembered for that successful little business though. He would eventually become known as one of the greatest showmen of all time.

He began by simply working on small projects outside of his store. Every day, he went in and managed his business, but in his free time, he explored new business ventures to figure out his passion.

That passion was sparked when he met a blind slave woman who claimed she was George Washington's nurse and was 161 years old. He knew it wasn't right, but her appearance was compelling. He decided to strike a deal to showcase her and that got him thinking of creating a museum. Although he had mixed success, he would build upon his idea, adding crazy and curious attractions such as a mermaid with the body of a monkey and a tail of a fish, and a four-year-old who claimed he was eleven (named Tom Thumb).

"Select the kind of business that suits your natural inclinations and temperament," Barnum said. "I never could succeed as a merchant. I have tried it unsuccessfully several times."

I have always grown up thinking that doing what you're good at is wrong and that you should do what you are passionate about. When I watched heroes talk about doing what they are passionate about, I felt that was what I should be doing: what I love.

Looking back though on all these heroes, I realized that they started with their inclinations before pursuing their passions.

You may stumble upon your inclinations early. Many people ignore them. Think about it. What are you really good at? What is it that takes you the least amount of effort to do, and yet you can do it so much better than everyone else?

If you don't know, you must search and explore. Don't go against your inclinations. What you must steal from these heroes is the view that there is *nothing wrong* with going with your strengths.

I go to work and I hate it, but I've come to realize that I am good at it and it allows me to pursue my passions.

You don't have to make your passion your job.

Channel these heroes when you don't feel like going to work or school. Perhaps you dislike what you're doing. Maybe you just want to do something more fun. You can dream of your passion as a form of living, but you need to concentrate on what you have at present.

Your inclinations give you a head start.

And a head start allows you to perfect the inclination faster than anyone else. This will then provide you the time and resources to delve into your passions.

12. ALWAYS STAY CURIOUS

Without curiosity, you won't be able to find what you may love or what you are passionate about. Worst of all, you may never realize your potential or find what you were meant for.

Heroes stay curious

When there is something that interests them, they explore it, which often leads them to find success or passion (or both).

Sam Zemurray wouldn't own a banana empire if he hadn't wondered what the men at the shipping docks were doing with bananas.

Albert Einstein would never have been able to come up with his theories if it weren't for his curiosity.

"I have no special talent," Einstein once said. "I am only passionately curious."

My game company, for example, was losing money and was not creating any successful games (most making less than $100). I decided to go to a games developer conference to check out what was trending. There I learned about a pair of goggles that took you into a virtual world.

Now called virtual reality, it was something novel and new then. I was curious and decided to learn more.

When I returned back home, I arranged a meeting with the team and told them it was time to change direction. Using a whiteboard, I explained the new technology and what we could do. We brainstormed for hours on our next game project.

Our project was the game I mentioned earlier, Crazy Fishing VR, and was our first of many games that helped bring the company out of near bankruptcy.

Without being curious, I never could have pivoted the company's direction. I had to find something new because what we had wasn't working.

So, stay curious.

BE CURIOUS ABOUT NEW THINGS

When Walt Disney learned about the introduction of Technicolor for motion pictures, he decided to add full-fledged color to his animations. By negotiating an exclusive contract with Technicolor's newly developed tricolor system (against his brother's wishes!), Disney was able to be at the forefront of showing cartoons and animations in color.

And he didn't stop there.

He wondered if a full-length, animated movie could be made. In typical Disney style, he decided to bet the studio on it.

His bet was on the first full-length animated film: *Snow White and the Seven Dwarfs*. Everyone thought it was going to fail. No one could convince him it was a stupid idea. Hollywood called it "Disney's Folly."

But Disney stayed confident.

When the film did come out, it earned $8.5 million in its initial release with a standing ovation. It had cost him two million to produce at the time.

Disney once said, "We keep moving forward, opening new doors, and doing new things, because we are curious—and curiosity keeps leading us down new paths."

Disney remained curious even when he was at the top. His company started to make money, but he continued down different paths (he pioneered adding sound to his animations).

Even when people tried to convince him that there was no point to his explorations, he kept going.

Keep opening new doors. If you can't find a door to open, then venture into the unknown and find new doors to explore.

ALWAYS REMAIN CURIOUS

Remaining curious isn't easy. How often do you "wonder" about something but never seek the answer? We often wonder but never follow through. If we leave our questions unanswered it may prevent us from finding success.

Heroes take their curiosity and run with it. They let the curiosity build, slowly growing into a storm, which creates a flash of inspiration. Whatever you're curious about, learn more about it. Find ways to go deeper.

Chip Conley, the founder of the legendary hotel group Joie De Vivre, said, "curiosity is the elixir of life." It explains why he was able to start the next chapter of his life and help run Airbnb as a strategic advisor.

By being curious, you open doors to places you never looked at before—and sometimes those are the very places where you need to be.

When Howard Shultz founded Starbucks, it wasn't because he was looking for good coffee.

In 1975 he was working as an appliance salesman at Hammerplast, a company that sold European coffee makers in the United States.

He had something that made him wonder though: Why was one particular company in Seattle buying so many coffee makers? Every month, the numbers went up.

Schultz remembers thinking, "I got to go to Seattle."

He booked a trip, and the moment he walked into a Starbucks, he felt at home. He knew he had to be a part of the company, and so he did all he could to join them.

A much similar story is shared by Ray Kroc. A man who was 52 years old, medically unwell, and an appliance salesman. The difference was he was selling paddle mixers for milkshakes. He heard that a hamburger stand in California had eight of his milkshake machines in constant operation, making forty shakes simultaneously. He was shocked. That level of productivity was unusual, so he went to check it out.

He drove his car up to the McDonald's hamburger restaurant and watched in awe as customers continued to line up. After that, he went into business with the brothers and launched the McDonald's franchise. He would eventually buy the company outright and, under his vision, he transformed McDonald's into a global franchise.

ASK YOURSELF HOW DOES IT WORK?

We could also look at the great Henry Ford, who always wanted to know how things worked, and every time he had the chance he would take things apart to study them. At first, it was watches, and then it was steam machines.

On one fateful day, he saw a car and realized it was extremely uncomfortable for the driver and passenger.

From that day on, he set about making an incredible car and went on to understand how the automobile worked. The only problem was he had no money. He took on a few jobs and formed a new company to build his own car. The company failed. This didn't deter Ford one bit. He went on to found another company, The Ford Motor Company.

Cars at the time were being raced, and consequently, they were built for speed. But Ford had another question to answer: *Why isn't there a car that everyone can afford?*

When his company started making different types of cars, there was one model, the famous Model T, which was easy to drive and repair.

That would be the beginning of the legacy Henry Ford started. He wanted to make the Model T and make it the standard for automobiles. He wanted to know if people would drive a car that was more easily maintainable and not just merely driving as fast as possible.

He kept asking the questions and seeking answers. How does the car work? How can the car be made more affordable? What type of vehicles do people want to buy?

You must do the same, continually asking questions and finding answers. *Don't let your curiosity go unanswered.*

You must find the answers to your questions. If another question arises, find the answer to that one as well. Curiosity is about questioning things and wondering. If at some moment you wonder, "What if?"—work to find the answer.

Curiosity allows you to open doors you would otherwise ignore. It is the one source of energy that will enable you to venture even further outside your comfort zone.

I sometimes find myself wondering something, and then just letting it fade away in my memory. Now, I act upon it immediately. If I have a question, I write it down. If I have an idea, I may quickly message a friend and ask if I can run something past her.

Don't let these wonderments go to waste. As your curiosity builds up, you may get a flash of inspiration like Henry Ford or Albert Einstein. You need to foster it.

When questions come to you, channel these heroes and remember that only good can come from curiosity. New passions. New people. New ventures.

Curiosity never killed the cat; it only made it stronger.

13. HAVE A CLEAR GOAL

Heroes have precise goals. But a goal alone isn't enough. Anyone can set a goal. You can tell yourself to lose weight. Open a business. Anyone can do that.

I've told myself plenty of times to lose weight. I told myself to write a book years before I started working on it.

To start doing something, you must at least have a rough idea of how you plan to get there. You can shoot for the stars, but without a map to get you to where you want to go, you don't have a chance. You need some guidance.

Kevin Hart wasn't just doing comedy for no reason. He wanted to eventually get the opportunity to perform for Lucien Hold (the man who could make him a star).

Gordon Ramsay didn't just open a Michelin star restaurant. He had always dreamed of opening one. To achieve it, Ramsay made a plan to train under the very best, and then, did just that.

The map doesn't have to be perfect, but the direction needs to be as clear as possible.

When I first set goals, I write them down and stick them up on my fridge. Every motivational book told me that was the way to do it. Although part of that is correct, having the goal was not enough. I knew what I wanted to do, but without planning how I was going to get there, I really didn't do anything.

Anyone can put a Post-It note up and write their goal on it. I had to determine what steps would lead me toward achieving my goal.

When I wanted to learn Chinese, I had to ask myself what steps were required. I ended up writing down the classes I would take and the books I needed to purchase. I signed up for night classes and stuck to a schedule.

Heroes don't stare at some idea or concept and wait. It doesn't matter if their first step is wrong; they adjust and keep going.

Definitely set goals, but make sure you take the first step of the journey and have a plan of how to get from here to there.

SHOOTING FOR SPACE

Chris Hadfield, the first Canadian to walk on the moon, had one goal: He wanted to be an astronaut.

"I wasn't destined to be an astronaut. I had to turn myself into one…"

When Chris was nine years old, he saw the Apollo 11 Moon landing televised on television. At that moment, he decided he wanted to do the same thing. At the time, only Americans were accepted into the space program, so he had no clue what to do. There was no program he could enroll in, no manual he could read.

He drafted a rough idea and started with getting into the air by joining the Royal Canadian Air Cadets.

At times, he almost strayed from his path. He considered joining a commercial airline, but his wife nudged him (this is why you need to surround yourself with supportive people), saying, "Don't give up on being an astronaut—I can't let you do that to yourself or to us. Let's wait just a little bit longer and see how things play out."

So, he thought again on where he needed to go next. What step would bring him closer to his goal?

He decided to be a test pilot and planned out the degree he needed so that when the Canadian Space Agency (CSA) started hiring, he would be prepared. He enrolled in university and studied aviation systems. When he completed his degree, it so happened that the CSA was looking for astronauts and he would be eligible to compete for the top spot.

Fate? Luck?

He only had that chance because he stayed focused on his goal. Among the 5,329 applications, he would make the top 500.

Then, the top 100.

After multiple medical exams and interviews, he was asked: "Do you want to be an astronaut?" With that, he would be the first Canadian to ever walk in space.

If you shoot for the stars, you better have a damn good plan on how to get there.

THE PRECISE LIST

Not many know this, but Arnold Schwarzenegger had written down a list of his goals. When he was studying, he made a very defined list that involved earning enough money to save $5000, to work out five days a week, and to find an apartment building to buy and move into.

"It might seem like I was handcuffing myself by setting such specific goals," Schwarzenegger wrote, "but it was actually just the opposite: I found it liberating. Knowing exactly where I wanted to end up freed me totally to improvise how to get there."

By creating a clear list of his goals, he achieved them all and more. He invested in an apartment complex and started a home order gym information business. He then eventually set his goal toward acting, beginning as a masseur on a television show. He took acting lessons and tried to talk to the right people to help start his career.

> *Clear goals aren't locking you down, they free you from distractions that keep you from moving toward those goals.*

Benjamin Franklin also had a written list of goals. Known as the Thirteen Virtues, Franklin made a list of the attributes he wanted to build. These virtues would add to his character, such as sincerity, frugality, and cleanliness. He didn't work on all of them at once, but instead chose one and worked on it each week. By making a defined list of traits he wanted to work on, he achieved it to the best of his ability.

HAVE A CLEAR GOAL

Be clear on what your goals are.

When Bear Grylls was walking around the Indian Himalayas, he had a vision to climb Mount Everest.

"Dreams, though, are cheap, and the real task comes when you start putting in place the steps needed to make those dreams reality."

To achieve his dream, he needed to build his stamina and athletic ability. So, he joined the Special Air Service (SAS). Although he failed to join the SAS the first time because he was too slow, he tried again and succeeded.

During his time with the SAS his parachute failed to open and he fell, fracturing his back (he shattered three vertebrae). Though his dream felt like it was fading away, he decided he wanted to make Everest happen, no matter what.

He didn't forget.

Grylls would spend time in the mountains carrying heavy rucksacks and preparing for his climb. But that alone was not enough; he needed some form of sponsorship. He was met with a lot of rejections (Richard Branson was one of them!), but he eventually found a deal to become one of the youngest to climb Mount Everest. He was determined to reach his goal. He worked on one objective with a clear plan that stayed with him through many obstacles and difficulties.

SO, WHAT ARE YOUR GOALS?

You don't have to write down your goals, but having a reminder of where you're headed and how you plan to achieve them is compulsory (and it won't do any harm either). It is inefficient to keep guessing about what you want to do. You might as well swim in the ocean in search of sunken treasure, without a map.

So, what are your goals? Are they written down? Do you have a rough idea of how you will get there?

You can't start unless you know where the beginning is. If you want to learn something, pick an online course and do it. If you have a business proposal, what is the fastest way for you to begin your venture?

Have a rough blueprint aimed at achieving what you want.

Steal from these heroes a concise way of setting your goals. Be clear and definite in what you want and create a map to get there. The plan may be loose and it can be flexible, but there are points of reference to your progression.

You need to know you are *consistently* moving in the right direction.

Three years ago, I told myself I would exercise. I was gaining fat and looked horrible. I was no longer taking care of myself. It took me a whole year before I even started.

Written on the wall was a piece of paper I have framed today: "Get fit." I never did.

Looking back, every day I told myself: Tomorrow, I will do it. Next week, I will get started.

What made me change my way of thinking was when I talked to a friend who is a personal trainer. He told me to write down the plan that was going to get me my results. I made a spreadsheet of the daily exercises I was going to do at the gym. I wrote down the food I would eat. I planned the exercises for months in advance. The goal was getting closer.

Clear goals and a clear plan are necessary to achieve what you want.

Twists and turns can happen in your journey: some good, others completely unpredictable. What keeps a hero going is the end goal. The finish line. That is what will matter most. You must possess an unflinching and clear conviction in your goal. You write it down and you stop at nothing to get there. You create paths that may not be present to you but are for others. If you hit an obstacle, you will find a way to go around it or break through it. You must have your own finish line.

When you set your goal, channel these heroes.

When you're unsure if something is right for your purpose, remember to ask yourself if it takes you in the right direction. You may get distracted (like when I get distracted playing games or going out). Nevertheless, you have to ask yourself if you're straying further and further from your goals.

So set a goal and make it as clear as possible. Map the known landmarks that get you to where you need to be. Go.

14. CARVE YOUR OWN PATH

Sometimes you're handed a life road map and told where to go. You aren't sure of your direction, so you take the script and go with it.

But how many people are happy living the life others expect of them?

The top regret voiced by people who are dying is that they lacked the courage to live a life true to themselves, and ended up living the life others expected of them. This common regret makes it easy to see how many dreams have gone unfilled.

Heroes refuse to take the script they are given. They carve out their own path.

IT'S YOUR CHOICE

Sometimes you're forced down a path. You're given an ultimatum: Do this or get out.

If Michael Dell had followed his family, all of them doctors, he would have never founded Dell Computers. As a freshman pre-med student, he built kits for computers, and then sold them. He realized he was onto a new business idea. Why not sell computers as a whole package? He did just that and started his company. By age 27, he would become the youngest C.E.O. in *Fortune*'s list of top 500 corporations. Dell would choose to go with what he believed to be his future. He didn't have to follow in his parent's footsteps. He carved out his own path.

On the corner of a block was a wannabe rapper who accepted that he would have to be a hustler for life, making a living by selling drugs.

He had witnessed too many rappers shot down by record corporations.

"I buried my little rap dreams," Jay-Z reminisced.

He had been arrested, witnessed gunfights, and sold crack. It was going to be an endless cycle. But one day, he realized that he sold crack to addicts who were killing themselves and collecting beaten up wrinkled bills. He finally asked himself, "What the f*** am I doing?"

He decided to change his path.

Jay-Z decided to model himself off his own hero. For him, that person was Russell Simmons. He realized that Russell was successful, even though he had never rapped a single bar in his life. Yet, Simmons was a pioneer in the music industry. He was creating a lifestyle of music, fashion, comedy, and film, and then selling it. Jay-Z wanted in.

Having been rejected by Columbia, Def Jam, and Uptown, Jay-Z decided to follow in Russell's footsteps. He would create his own record company. He called it Roc-A-Fella Records. The independent label would grow, and so Jay-Z was on his own path to success.

It started out with Jay-Z's first album. After producing several hits, the album succeeded and created an impact within the hip-hop community.

Jay-Z changed the road that he was on. He *chose* it. It was in his control.

You are capable of controlling yours. You decide when you veer off it. Go for the best.

PARENTS' PATHWAY OR THE HIGHWAY

We can't blame our parents for giving us a script. They want the best for us. But there should be nothing stopping us from attempting to create something of our own. After all, only we know what works for us.

Walt Disney was told by his father to stop doing cartoons. His dad suggested he work at a jelly factory, to get a "real job."

"I don't want to work at the jelly factory," Disney replied. "I want to be an artist."

His father was shocked. It made no sense to him.

"You can't make a living drawing pictures. You need a real job!"

Even at a young age, Disney was passionate and persistent. "I'll get a real job, as a newspaper cartoonist!" He walked away, leaving his father speechless.

Walt Disney was going to prove he could make it as an artist. Even though his journey was a difficult one, full of betrayal and failure, he succeeded. He was determined to make it. He carved out his path.

We may never have had Mickey Mouse if Disney worked at the jelly factory.

James Caan, a successful entrepreneur, was told by his father to stay in the family business. He would be groomed to be part of the company and everything would be smooth sailing for him.

It didn't turn out that way.

He didn't say goodbye to his parents. He planned his departure and found a job as a sales rep. He barely got by, and to save money he would eat cornflakes till payday.

Although the family business was the easiest option—free car, salary, and financial security—Caan wanted to know what it was like to make it on his own.

But it was not like Caan knew what to do. He remained active in his job hunting, found a recruitment job, and began to save money. He realized his strengths and formed a new recruitment company called Alexander Mann. He eventually sold the company and continued to fund new companies. He also starred on *Dragon's Den*, a television show where participants invest in innovative businesses presented by founders.

Alan Sugar did very much the same as Caan. Sugar is a business magnate who founded an electronics company when electronics were on the rise.

Early in his life, he stated, "I'm going to start working for myself."

His father looked at him as if he were mad. "What do you mean, you're going to work for yourself? Who is going to pay you on Friday?"

Alan replied that he was going to pay himself on Friday.

His plan of action? Borrow some money, buy a second-hand minivan and sell electronic gear. It sounded simple enough.

The following day, he sprang into action. He did exactly as he planned. He started selling electrical goods out of the truck, such as radio aerials for cars and other electronic products.

It was during this venture that he spotted a niche market for turntable covers (used to protect turntables from dust). He invested money into an injection mold machine to make cheap but effective covers. He started finding his own path. He would later add additional hi-fi goods that followed the same principle: Cheap but cost effective.

After expanding his business, his company would grow into an international exporter and importer of electronic goods. Not bad for someone who decided to carve his own path.

SO, START CARVING

I am reminded when I listen to these stories that my parents wanted me to have a safe path. Study well, get a good-paying job, and you will be okay.

I can't disagree. It makes sense. Wouldn't you want that for your own child? But when I told them I wanted to start my own company, they couldn't understand why. Why risk things when you already have a steady paycheck?

Nevertheless, I realized I needed to carve my own path.

It certainly wasn't easy. Sometimes when I needed financial support, I wouldn't get it, because I was going against the grain.

Heroes who chose to make their own path do it on their own.

Eventually, once I started showing stability, my parents warmed up to my idea. They were even starting to talk about it with friends and family. One day I even overheard my parents tell their friends that I was running a successful medical business and were proud of me.

Even though they were against it initially, by carving out my own path they learned to accept and even respect it.

It can difficult for others at first, but you need to make your own story.

What we must steal from these heroes is the courage to begin carving our own path. There is no time for regret.

You don't want to be on your deathbed wishing you had lived life the way you wanted.

These heroes didn't accept the situation they were in. Instead, they started to envision and formulate a plan that allowed them to create their own route. Some heroes just went with it; they set off on the road not taken.

If you're set on carving your own path, be clear and have *conviction*, like these heroes. But know this: Carving your own path is certainly not for the faint of heart. Be ready for the challenge that will await you. Once you're prepared, there is no need to turn back. Step forward with courage and carve away.

15. DO ONE THING DAMN WELL

There are advantages to doing one thing really well, but it is a challenging task. Today, it is getting harder and harder to master any one thing. Distractions. Choices. The list is endless.

As technology advances, mastery becomes more difficult. We seem to expect shortcuts. We want things now. But without attaining mastery, that's not going to happen. You cannot become an expert tennis player like Andre Agassi overnight. Beethoven did not become a legendary composer within a few weeks. Such mastery takes time.

Heroes not only concentrate on one thing, they also ensure they exhaust every step they can take to perfect it.

Can you do one thing really well?

All of your heroes do *one* thing very well. You may look at Virgin and say: Richard Branson does everything! Planes, entertainment, and gymnasiums. Yet if you take an in-depth look into these companies, you find that Richard Branson started in record players and concentrated solely on music.

Jeff Bezos, who created Amazon as the "everything store," started with books and then, eventually, e-books before creating Amazon.

Not all heroes know straight away what they want. Some are lucky and figure it out early in their lives. The difference with heroes is that the moment they *have* figured out what they want, they dive so deep into it, they become the masters and pioneers of that very field.

YOU MUST TRY NEW THINGS TO FIND YOUR ONE THING

In your search to find what that *one* thing is, remember that heroes remain proactive and continually try new things to determine what they will dive into.

Take Milton Hershey. He first tried his hand at printing. Early on, he chanced to lean over to look at the machines and his hat fell into the machinery. Noises were heard and the system stopped. The owner looked at him in disgust and yelled to him, "Tell your father you are useless!" Hershey ran home in dismay and it was then that he decided to learn about making candy.

But what costs were incurred while Hershey was figuring out what he wanted?

Failed business ventures, family members banishing him, and a lot of wasted money, just to name a few.

Hershey had exhausted all his options. He tried many different types of candy, from cough drops to taffy and caramels (he got to chocolate much later).

In Hershey's second business attempt, he concentrated on taffy and caramels. He mastered the craft and learned that adding milk to caramels resulted in a much smoother consistency and delicious taste.

Although the venture started well, the situation soon became familiar: Once again, he ran out of money.

As he boarded the train heading home one day, he realized what he needed to do. But first, he needed money.

He went to his uncle and told him, "I think I now know how to make the candy business work. It's not about making a whole lot of things but making one thing well."

His uncle looked at him in disgust and told him to leave and never come back. As Hershey walked away, he thought, "It is all up to me now. I won't need much. A small shed, a way to pay freight on my equipment, and a whole lot of work. I'm smarter now. I know I can earn a good living making caramels."

Caramels were his choice. Caramels were his one thing that he would concentrate on.

Milton did eventually get the support he needed from a very close friend. Back in those days, there were no electronics. So, Milton only had a coal stove, metal kettles, and physical thermometers. On freezing cold days, Hershey would spend his time perfecting the temperature to ensure each pot was set correctly to allow the sugar to caramelize. He worked day and night on it—this was going to be his breakthrough that would lead to his first big success.

In Gary Keller's *The One Thing*, we learn that by concentrating on a single goal, we can obtain it. "Success is sequential," Keller writes, "not simultaneous."

By sticking to one thing, we can see it to the end and perfect it.

WORK AND HONE YOUR CRAFT

When Kevin Hart talks about his choice to go into comedy, his single goal was to keep performing to find the one man that would get him through the door and make it big: Lucien Hold.

To meet Lucien, Hart would perform over and over again with this hope. Some nights he would be booed and other nights the crowd was completely silent. But he kept going to more and more comedy clubs to perfect his craft. No matter where it was or if there was a small or large crowd, if he could perform, he did.

But when Hart finally met Lucien (who found Chris Rock and Jerry Seinfeld) and performed for him, Hart's performance was a bust. In fact, Lucien told him he should quit and find another profession—comedy was not for him.

What did Hart do? He doubled down. He wanted to perfect his art.

"So as long as you have the get-up-and-go to just do, and never stop, then you'll be fine," he said.

It did take Hart time to perfect his own comedy style, which would propel his career. His persistence paid off.

Initially, Hart centered his act on imitations of his personal heroes. Later on he delved into his own rhythm to hone his skills, and it wasn't until then that Hart was able to find his success.

He didn't deviate. He didn't get distracted. He worked endlessly on his craft. He worked on one thing and made sure he did it damn well.

What we must steal from these heroes is the ability to first search for our one thing. You can't rely on someone to tell you what you're good at or to just stumble upon it. You must try new things. You can't find the one thing if you don't attempt as many new ideas as you can.

How did Daymond John, founder of FUBU, stumble upon his idea of making clothes for fans of rap music? By trying new business ventures.

How did the original concept of Netflix start? By brainstorming new ideas (shampoos and baseball bats were part of the brainstorm!).

You can't stumble upon something unless you're actually moving. So, get moving. Keep searching until something hits.

Once you find out that one thing—double down. Perfect it. Throw all your energy into it.

Heroes know that they have a finite amount of time to become a master in the field. You must use whatever time you have available to make yourself a master of your one thing. Set yourself out to do something—then do it.

When I struggle to concentrate, get distracted, or find myself bored with what I'm working on, I channel my heroes. I realize that it's human to get distracted or lose interest. But I also remind myself that these heroes were human too, but they focused on *one* thing to reach their goal and dreams.

I might be looking at social media. I might be watching a television show or playing computer games, when really, I should be writing my book. As I write this chapter, I'm tempted to get distracted.

No matter what the thing is, there can only be one thing you concentrate on at a time. Multi-tasking doesn't exist. When you find yourself deviating from that one thing, or no longer searching, or standing still, channel these heroes.

Remind yourself that to become good or to find what you can succeed in, you must concentrate on one thing and be damn good at it.

16. SAY YES!

When an opportunity pops up, do you say yes?

I have said no to fantastic opportunities, with much regret. An interview for a job, a chance to expand my network—I convinced myself not to go. If someone opens a door for you and your immediate answer is no, accept the fact that you may never have a chance like that again.

You will make excuses or find reasons to not do something. Self-sabotage is common and very dangerous. You must say *yes* to excellent opportunities, *then* decide how to make that yes happen. Someone might find a job for you or try to help you achieve your goal. When they do, you must say yes!

BREAKING FEAR

In Shonda Rhimes's famous TED Talk, Rhimes, the creator of *Grey's Anatomy* and *Scandal*, decided to say yes to anything that scared her for one year. Public speaking, appearing on television, and acting were frightening to her, but this time she said yes.

What happened? They no longer scared her. She even started to enjoy them, and it changed her life.

There are many times we let fear override us.

Even today, I think of a time when I was about to speak at a small conference, and as I walked toward the hall, I started to tell myself it wasn't worth it, that I could quit and pretend I was sick. It was a stupid way of thinking.

Don't let fear hold you back.

Tina Fey said, "Greet everything with 'yes'."

And why did she say that? Because the longer she thought about any new opportunity, the more she could convince herself not to do it. By greeting everything presented with "yes," she didn't give herself time to reconsider. She simply had to deliver.

When she was offered a job as head writer at *Saturday Night Live*, she didn't think; she said yes straight away. Although she was living in Chicago and wasn't sure about moving to New York, she went with it because it was a massive opportunity. She said yes even though she was afraid of the responsibility.

> *This isn't to say you should aimlessly say yes. There's a difference between saying yes to an opportunity and saying yes because you think it will make someone happy.*

YES MEN

Ben Horowitz, a cofounder of Andreesen Horowitz and a successful entrepreneur, was once asked how he was able to work effectively across three companies over eighteen years. His answer related to creating an environment that allowed people to challenge each other and provide critical feedback.

There's something special about knowing that the person you're working with isn't challenging you to pull you down but instead is trying to improve you or your idea. No yes-man is going to achieve that for you.

Even today, Ben says that his business partner (Marc Andreesen) still upsets him almost every day in questioning his thinking—but it still works.

The same could be said about Abraham Lincoln. When he formed his presidential cabinet, he famously filled it with his rivals. They were men who were considered the brightest and best minds in the country, and they were unafraid to challenge Lincoln and assert their opposition. Lincoln welcomed it, believing that having the best and not yes-men would provide a much higher benefit to the country and to him.

This is similar to Pixar's Braintrust: Everyone is honest and working toward the same goal. No one holds back and all try to solve a problem together. By being candid with each other, they can be genuine and work to find the *best* result.

Don't surround yourself with yes-men. Surround yourself with the very best people who want a similar goal.

SUCCESS FROM A YES

Bob Iger was once told he would have to become head of ABC Entertainment in Los Angeles. He was living in New York at the time and only had experience in sports and news. The change was a curveball, but it was a possible opportunity to try something new.

Although he would have to relocate, it was an opportunity that would help him climb up in the company. He said yes, made the move with the family, and started work. In four years, he became the president of the ABC Network Television Group.

Disney would later acquire ABC, and because Iger had gained invaluable experience, he became a suitable candidate for the CEO position. His experience was created because Iger said yes to opportunities. And that led him to becoming the CEO of Disney.

Do you know who *Doctor Yes* is? That's the nickname of Richard Branson, founder of Virgin.

"If somebody offers you an amazing opportunity, but you aren't sure you can do it, say yes! Then learn how to do it later!"

Branson always said yes when it came to a new opportunity. When he found a new idea, he would immediately say yes and go with—and consequently founded Virgin.

So, when an opportunity presents itself, say yes. Don't let it go to waste. It may never come back.

Significant opportunities are missed because you spend too long thinking about if you should walk through the door.

Instead, just walk through and decide from there.

When in doubt, channel and steal from these heroes. Take from them the power of "yes."

Yes, in the face of fear.

Yes, in the face of opportunity.

17. DON'T MISS THE BIG WAVES

Opportunities come in waves. Some waves are enormous; others are small. Some you may never see coming because you aren't looking.

Heroes are always looking.

How did Steve Jobs form Apple? Because he seized on a small opportunity when a store owner gave him a new idea to sell pre-made computer kits.

How did J.R.R. Tolkien end up finishing his book, *The Hobbit*, and then start writing *The Lord of the Rings*? Because a publisher had heard that Tolkien had an unfinished children's story. Tolkien had lent the typescript of *The Hobbit* to one of his students who provided a copy to a publisher, Stanley Unwin. Stanley's ten-year-old son loved the book and wanted a completed copy (an eerily similar story to Harry Potter!). The moment a publisher was interested, Tolkien immediately got to work finishing *The Hobbit*. He finished the book, and it was published within a month, and by the end of the year, the first edition sold out completely.

Heroes seize an opportunity once it is presented to them.

I have never forgotten the opportunities I've missed.

A friend once asked me to join a startup business development company and I refused simply because I was afraid and had no clue what to do. I missed a wave. My friend's company is still kicking today.

Another time, I was offered to invest in a little café my friend wanted to start. I didn't because I felt it was a silly idea. He now runs a successful board game café in Melbourne.

Opportunities come and go, and I have missed many. When you are given one, don't let it go. You never know when it will come again (if at all).

MUSICIAN TO PROGRAMMER

Derek Sivers was a professional musician but wasn't popular enough to get a distributor to sell his CDs online. At the time, there was no easy-pay options for online sales, and no way to whip up a website over a weekend.

He had a problem and he needed a solution.

He taught himself programming, and with trial and error created a website with a giant buy button. He told some of his friends and musicians who had the same problem, and they wanted in. He realized he was onto something, an opportunity, which he seized! He found a niche that wasn't occupied and immediately set to work.

Sivers went to a bookstore and learned more about PHP and MYSQL (programming languages). But the most significant wave came when iTunes was announced. iTunes was a game changer—it would create a platform for musicians to sell their music directly to consumers.

Sivers noticed another opportunity: He could list the musicians on iTunes. He met with Steve Jobs and received a contract from Apple to upload music onto iTunes.

Investors started getting interested in his project, and though he still worked in a back tape room to earn a living, he grew this small project into a full-fledged company. Sivers jumped onto the wave that would lead him to success. Today, CD Baby has paid over a total of $700 million to artists alone.

When you think you have an idea and an opportunity, seize it immediately.

CREATING A BANANA EMPIRE

Sam Zemurray, nicknamed "Sam the Banana Man," emigrated to America when he was 14 years old, with no formal education. Coming from a poor family, Sam tried to make as much money as he could. He did odd jobs and sold iron, chicken, and pigs to make a living. But his life changed when he had an encounter with a banana…

He was walking by the shipping docks and watched as bananas were taken off the boats. He saw how the best ones were selected and then transported to stores. The process was pure manpower from quality inspection of the bananas to loading the good green bananas on an air-cooled, straw-filled car.

Sam continued to observe this process daily, until a question struck him: What about the discarded and "not so good" bananas?

He examined the process, ignoring the green bananas, and instead, noted the sizeable pile of discarded bananas, not good enough quality to ship to stores. The growing pile consisted of overripe bananas in various stages of yellow and brown.

He asked himself again: What about these bananas, were they just going to waste?

After the trucks left with the green bananas, he walked down to the pier to talk to the dock men. Then, using his savings of one hundred and fifty dollars, he negotiated to buy all the discarded bananas.

It was an opportunity. But now he had a new problem: He had to sell them.

Time was of the essence. Every passing moment meant the bananas kept ripening. Sam rushed to the train station, rented a slat-sided railcar for the one-way trip to Lower East Side Manhattan after the bananas were brought to the docks for loading.

But the situation got worse. The train was going to be delayed, further threatening his investment, but he hatched a plan and sent a telegraph ahead, telling local merchants what he had to sell and that they would get a percentage of the sales.

He made a plan, on the spot, and it worked. In doing so, the moment he arrived, with extremely ripe bananas on his back, he was able to sell every single one and still end up with a profit.

Sam saw an opportunity and went for it.

NO DIRECTION MEANS MORE OPPORTUNITIES

Marc Cuban initially had no idea what he would do. He was unemployed and heading to Dallas with absolutely zero job prospects. He started out as a bartender.

While working, he saw an ad in the newspaper to sell computer software at a retail store. He pulled out a grey suit and applied for the job. To make sure he had enough knowledge, he took home different software material every day and read it. He spent extra time learning as much as he could as he saw the rise of computers and wanted to get ahead.

"I had nothing. So, I had nothing to lose, right?"

Cuban would then go on to start his own software business, Microsolutions. That was the beginning of his entrepreneurial adventure. He would later sell the company for $6 million.

In contrast, Felix Dennis, author of *How to Be Rich,* had many missed opportunities in technology. When the personal computer industry grew, he thought of making a magazine about personal computers.

Felix thought of jumping onto the opportunity. However, when he told everyone, the responses were negative. People advised him that nobody would ever pay money to read monthly magazines about dinky little computers.

Felix gave up the idea.

Shortly thereafter, another entrepreneur launched a magazine called *Personal Computer World* that soon became a success. It was Felix's idea, but someone else executed it. Felix would later end up having to buy this magazine at a premium, much to his regret.

> *Don't let yourself miss an opportunity—it may only come once.*

When we have a light bulb moment, how many of us actually act on it? We're all guilty of having flashes of inspiration and ignoring them. But even if we do notice them, the worst mistake we make is *not acting on them fast enough.*

Have you had an idea and waited too long and ended up forgetting it? You had a little bit of extra energy and didn't use it?

Heroes take this inspiration and push themselves to commit.

Whether your goal is a new business idea or deciding to make a website, take your inspiration and act on it as soon as possible. Don't wait. You make sure the next step is happening regardless.

Derek Sivers found a problem and decided to act upon it.

Ray Kroc realized that the McDonald's brothers were onto something and saw the future of fast food.

You see an opportunity, and you take it. Start to formulate a plan and go with it the moment you can.

When I'm presented with an opportunity, I try not to hesitate. I still find it difficult, but I channel these heroes and realize that I *must* take every opportunity and grab my advantage.

If you find a wave, something that will push you closer to achieving your dreams, you *have* to ride it. Opportunities have been missed and regretted. Don't let one slip by. Seize it.

When you feel something could get big, measure your risks, and jump into it. When you think you have a new idea, start the plan, and execute it. You don't need to risk your life or spend all your life savings.

You just need to take advantage—now.

18. GET TO THE POINT OF NO RETURN

Heroes set goals that seem unrealistic. They put themselves in positions that just seem impossible. Much like Caesar's crossing of the Rubicon River, where his army was to either triumph or he was to be executed, heroes put themselves in a point of no return. You face either success or failure. That is your choice. You don't get to sit in the middle; you are forced into an answer.

Also, there's the fable of the donkey stuck between two bales of hay that dies of starvation because he fails to make a choice. Heroes put themselves into these positions as often as possible. They don't sit in the middle. Since failure is part of the process for success, then either one is beneficial.

You must either triumph or fail.

I have enjoyed sitting in the middle because it is comfortable. If you don't need to make a choice, then why not delay it indefinitely?

I remember a client coming to the company and asking if the team could make an app for him. His time frame was short. I didn't think it was possible, but it was going to benefit the team greatly. If we stretched it or if I hired a few more freelancers, it could be done. I told him I would get back to him.

I sat on the fence.

I have no doubt if I told him we could do it and then immediately started planning we could have made the app. In a few weeks, he found someone else who did just that. His app now has made one of my competitors a lot of money, and I definitely regret not committing there and then. I lost an opportunity and a chance at success.

Sometimes you have to burn the ships, so that you're past the point of no return. I didn't burn the ships. I never got off the damn boat in the first place.

I CAN DO IT… SORT OF

When Kerry Stokes landed in Australia, he had no clue what to do. The flights were sporadic then and he was stuck in Western Australia for a week. As he walked around, he noticed that television was becoming a massive phenomenon. Electrical stores and businesses were busy. He wanted in.

The question was: How would he do it? How does a person with no degree or skill set do it on his own in a city he doesn't know too well?

He pretended he knew how to install televisions. He had no skill at all and had no idea how to install TVs, but he had to get his foot in the door. He applied for a job and said he could do everything. At the time, he had absolutely no clue how to do any of it. Although they wanted him to start straight away, he told them he needed three days.

He already crossed the river, and now there was no way to return. Either he was going to learn how to install a television or they were going to find out he was a phony.

He rushed to the library and learned as much as he could for three days straight. The coming Monday, he was given keys, tools, ladder, and cables for attaching aerials onto the roofs of houses.

No one knew any better.

It isn't the first time someone said they could do something when, in actual fact, they had no idea of their next plan of action. But these people still delivered.

Perhaps it was Kerry's belief that he could, and the deadline he gave himself helped him achieve it.

Jerry Weintraub was considered one of the greatest showmen of all time by getting Elvis on tour.

How was that possible?

Every morning he would call Elvis's manager. And every morning he was rejected. He was told that he would never be the one who got to promote Elvis.

After a year, Jerry's persistence paid off, but he was given an ultimatum. The deal would be done if Jerry had a million dollars by the next day. A whole million—in cash.

Forget the fact he kept calling for an entire year, how was he going to produce a million dollars? What was his response?

"Okay, I'll get it, and I'll be there."

Jerry didn't have a million dollars stored away. He actually owed the bank $65,000. But he convinced himself he would get it.

He called everyone he knew in show business and outside of it. Some told him he was on drugs. Others thought he must have been smoking something out of this world. But he didn't give up.

Two hours before the meeting, a lawyer he had called said he knew of a big Elvis fan who might be willing to put in the million dollars. The connection pulled through.

Somehow, Jerry got the money. Luck? Possibly. But chance only came to him because he said yes. He was either going to get the million or not. Success or fail. The point of no return.

Through thick and thin, he became Elvis's first promoter, which skyrocketed his success.

Similarly, Sal Khan was meeting with an education board to pitch his idea of Khan Academy. When they asked him if his program would work on Macs, his response was, "Of course!" But it didn't. He didn't own a Mac and had no idea if his software would run on one.

After the meeting, he went straight to his local computer store and brought a MacBook. Khan pulled an all-nighter, hacking and making his program compatible with Macs (Sal Khan was not a programmer mind you; he worked in finance!).

These heroes said yes and made it work. They tested their limits and achieved their potentials. They were willing to risk it because they knew it was an opportunity they could not miss.

JAIL OR SUCCESS

Richard Branson, the founder of Virgin, had a mail-order business that was losing money. Although the company was growing, the money was nowhere to be seen. Branson analyzed the ongoing costs and knew it would be impossible to make money. The company was selling records too cheap and the costs to run the company were eating away any money they made. However, he noticed that if he didn't pay tax when purchasing the vinyl records, he could be entirely out of debt.

He decided he had to do it, but he would pay the price.

The customs officials had caught on and planned to raid Virgin.

They locked Branson in a jail cell.

"I vowed to myself that I would never do anything that would cause me to be imprisoned," Branson says, reflecting on that moment. But this gave him a push that allowed Virgin to succeed. They gave him an ultimatum: If he didn't pay off his debt and the tax owed, he would go to jail.

It was make or break. He worked twice as hard, and because of the team he surrounded himself with, everyone chipped in to make sure Branson made the repayments.

Heroes make attempts and willingly do anything to achieve what they can. Branson almost paid the price. You don't need to do illegal things, but when you're pushed to either succeed or fail, you never know what you can achieve.

When have you told someone you couldn't do something they asked, but they let you do it anyway because they believed in you? And then, when you do it, you actually achieve it?

I have wondered when it is wrong to promise and fail to deliver. The answer I have found is that it's wrong when someone else's reputation and success depend on it.

Heroes stake their *own* reputation. The only person who is affected when they fail is themselves. If they fail, they will be responsible for it. They will wear the scars.

If a colleague needs help and you know someone for the job, give them a recommendation. If they insist you should do it, then create the right expectations. With that, you can attempt to do the very best and try to succeed. And much like these heroes, you may find out you can do it, after all.

Channel these heroes when you're stuck making a choice. Push yourself to do it. If the decision is between success or failure, see it as success or a free lesson. Stake your reputation. Cross the river and don't look back. Come back triumphant or with battle scars that will one day be a story you can tell.

19. DON'T HOLD GRUDGES

When someone betrays you, what do you do? How do you act when someone has taken your trust and used it against you?

I have found it difficult to get past betrayal. When I grew my first business, a medical-dental practice in Australia, I had reached a plateau. The business was earning the same amount each year, and I was exhausted. I had run the company for almost five years, and I felt it was time to move on. I sold the business to a nearby competitor. I made the decision because he was someone who was friendly and had the same vision of expanding the company. A few months later, I became a contractor for the business, and everything was running smoothly.

Or so I thought.

What I didn't realize was that he had included a particular clause in my contract. He was able to terminate my agreement with a one-month advance notice. If he did so, I would no longer be able to open a similar business or work within a specified distance.

He had a plan and was waiting to strike.

On a day I was about to go on holiday, he called me to his office and said, "I don't think we can work together anymore."

I was confused and shocked. I tried to tell him it was a bad idea. We talked but got nowhere.

I felt betrayed and got angry. I decided to just walk out and accept my fate. I was no longer allowed to work in the city and was going to be out of a job. Honestly, it took me months to mentally get over it.

In those months I was doing nothing. I wasted time fueling my anger.

Holding my grudges in fact moved me backward. I didn't think of the future anymore. My sleep was a mess. I didn't want to talk to anyone. I lost many opportunities along the way.

I let this person's betrayal get to me and instead of me moving forward, I allowed him to keep getting ahead.

Don't be me.

What heroes can do is move pass a grudge. They don't seek revenge. They accept the betrayal, learn from it, and move on, better prepared for the next opportunity. They don't waste precious time rehashing or speculating on what ifs.

It is often said that success is the best form of revenge. Heroes do that: They succeed to a point where the betrayal is forgotten.

When Marc Cuban started one of his first businesses, he had his receptionist cash the company's checks. He would later find out that the receptionist had whited out the company's name and put them under her own name. She banked $83,000 of $85,000 as her own money. Although he was angry, he admitted that "no one was going to cover my obligations but me."

He overcame the financial loss and didn't hold onto his anger and resentment, eventually selling the company for $6 million dollars.

SUCCESS IS REALLY THE BEST REVENGE

Sam Walton, the founder of Walmart, originally owned a small chain store called Ben Franklin. To start the store, he signed leases and borrowed money. While running the store, he realized he could save costs by cutting out the middlemen involved in purchasing products he planned to sell. He always sought the greatest value to pass on to customers.

In two and a half years, he would pay back all the money he had borrowed to start the store. In five years, his business was thriving. It was initially grossing $70,000 but was now grossing $250,000.

That five-year mark also meant the lease was up. The owner of the building didn't want to renew. So they gave Walton a price so high that they forced him to leave. Walton hated it, but they had successfully kicked him out.

What was their intention? To simply take over his business and keep it for themselves.

Did he mull over it? Of course. The difference, however, is that he didn't do it for long. As Sam says, "The challenge at hand was simple enough to figure out: I had to pick myself up and get on with it, do it all over again, only even better this time."

His next step was to look for another store and apply the lessons from his previous venture. The store would be called Walmart. Through expansions and building more and more stores, Sam would succeed in building an empire.

Perhaps not intentionally, he placed a Walmart near the location he was first kicked out of. The customers voted with their feet: The person who had run him out of town had to shut down.

Success really is the best revenge.

PEOPLE CAN STEAL FROM YOU

Early on in Nikola Tesla's career, he had created the arc-lighting system for two businessmen. The first thing they did was create a new company, and then forced Tesla to assign the patents to the new company. They abandoned him to form a new firm. Since the system Tesla created didn't need improvement, Tesla was no longer needed.

Tesla was without a job and no longer in a position to use his own inventions. All his efforts became useless and he fell on severely hard times, even being reduced to digging ditches.

"I lived through a year of terrible heartaches and bitter tears," he reflected.

Even so, Tesla was able to file a patent application of his own for a thermomagnetic motor. He worked on more inventions and understood his mistakes.

A crucial turning point for him was when he met Charles Peck and Alfred

Brown, who would help him perfect his AC motor. This new type of electromagnetic induction allowed him to sell his patent to Westinghouse in a deal that was financially lucrative.

Tesla did not give up. He kept working and doing jobs he hated just so he could work on his next invention.

People may steal from you. They make take whatever helps in their success.

Don't let them steal your future as well. Keep moving forward.

DON'T INVEST INTO REVENGE

Let's take a look at how Nike was formed.

Phil Knight, the founder, was in a tough position. The long story short is that Nike had a supplier for their shoes, Oni (shortened from Onitsuka), that had started ignoring Nike's orders.

Under new management, Oni's new leader, Kitami, was in touch with other distributors. Kitami wanted out and was looking for better distributors, and it was clear to him that Nike was not worth it.

The next time Phil and Kitami met, Kitami demanded to buy out 51% of Nike. The arrangement so far was that Nike distributed the shoes and Oni manufactured them. But Kitami was no longer happy with Nike and offered an ultimatum: Sell Nike or Oni would find new distributors. If Phil was reluctant to sell, Oni would no longer provide them shoes.

It was a lose-lose situation.

This was the moment of truth for Nike. Phil needed to create a new plan and fast. He knew for too long he had relied on Oni and needed to own the manufacturing himself. Betrayal was happening in front of him.

But instead of considering revenge or thinking of Kitami or remembering one of his best friends siding with Kitami, he concentrated on his company and on how he could succeed.

What Knight planned was to combine with another Japanese trading company and shoe manufacturer to create Nike's own shoes. In doing so, there was a turn in their fortunes.

Although the company morale was clearly gloomy, he organized a staff meeting and said bravely, "This is the moment we've been waiting for. Our moment. No more selling someone else's brand," Knight said. "What we need is a brand we can control because we have everything else, the shoes, the top runners. This is the *best thing* that could have ever happen to us."

They would redesign the shoe, and that was when the inimitable tick or "swoosh" was invented. It was the real start of Nike.

Knight dove deeper into building his company. Instead of seeking revenge or thinking of Oni's betrayal, he worked on succeeding—and he did just that.

Betrayal is something that can linger for a long time. I have let deception prevent me from doing some of the most amazing things in my life. Meeting new people. Forming new partnerships. Starting new ideas.

Holding onto grudges can prevent you from having your own success. When I meet friends scarred by past experiences, I'm reminded of my own. The people who get past them *learn* from these experiences and don't let grudges hold them back from starting again and succeeding.

We must accept that we will encounter people who will betray us. We will encounter people who believe that for them to succeed, someone must fall or fail. Or perhaps they just don't want you to succeed, and so, try to drag you down.

You must ignore the urge to seek revenge. Your success is by far the best revenge.

What we steal from these heroes is the strength to ignore the urge for revenge and to channel that energy into finding a path to success.

Channel these heroes when your thoughts fall onto the people who have betrayed you or the grudges you may hold. Don't let those thoughts affect your path to success.

Concentrate on the goal and tasks at hand. Use your energy to create a new plan for new successes.

20. REJECTION IS A GOOD THING

There isn't a single hero who hasn't gone through some form of rejection. Heroes accept that rejection is part of the process. Without rejection, you will never be able to achieve your goals.

What separates heroes is how they respond to that rejection.

Charlie Chaplin was told to give up acting. Elon Musk was booted from his C.E.O. position at PayPal. Even Steve Jobs was thrown out of his own company, Apple.

But how did they all respond?

By continually moving forward. Emotion may have initially affected them, but they didn't let the rejection get to them. They moved on as fast as they could.

As Musk said it best, "Life is too short for long-term grudges."

Rejection is often portrayed as a negative experience. It's understandable. It never feels good to be rejected. Even heroes aren't immune to emotional pain, but what makes them heroes is that they don't let a bad experience affect their next decision. They learn from that experience. They don't let rejections hold them back. They move on and keep pursuing what they want.

Chaplin kept believing and found his niche. Musk went on to create Tesla. Jobs went on to create a new company called NeXT.

Heroes don't stand still. They keep moving even in the face of rejection.

ONE DOOR CLOSES ANOTHER ONE OPENS

Jia Jiang once walked into a fast-food chain store and asked for unlimited burger refills and was immediately rejected. He asked Krispy Kreme to create five interlinked donuts. He even asked if he could make an announcement on a commercial airline.

Jiang was trying to get rejected. He simply wanted to prove that there's no harm in being rejected.

What Jiang realized through his journey of *purposely* getting rejected was that when he let his fear overtake him, he would hold back and ended up feeling full of regret. He allowed the fear of rejection to prevent him from doing what he wanted most. It is why he went on a quest to make outrageous requests.

"If something can't hurt me, then why should it scare me?" Jiang said in his book, *Rejection Proof*.

The most crucial turnaround in Jiang's journey was when he realized people don't *want* to reject you. It is not like people want to go out there and reject people for fun. It's not a great feeling *being* the one doing the rejecting. If you ask someone, they will try to do whatever they can to help you.

When Jiang asked to stay at a luxury hotel for free, he was immediately turned down, but he would then ask for a tour and was allowed to even nap on one of the hotel's beds. When he asked to slide down a fire pole, the fire department said no, but he would get a tour and ride in a fire truck instead.

Jiang realized that although you may get rejected for your idea or your requests, you may also encounter new avenues to explore. By actively being open to rejection, you may gain perspectives to open new paths for you.

You don't have to purposely get rejected, but the thought of rejection should not be what holds you back.

> *Behind every rejection is something you can learn, and it helps you find a route that will work for you. Rejection is a positive experience that comes from being openly curious.*

You just have to ask.

For you to succeed in achieving your goals, you must experience rejection. It is inevitable. Embrace that as part of the process. It will help you uncover the path that is meant for you.

Rejection is simply the world telling you that this path won't work. This person can't help you. This road is taken; find another path.

There have been times I let rejection take the better part of me. Most of the time when this happens, you're left wondering what *could* have happened. Accept that you may never know the answer because that moment has passed. That wave might only come once in a blue moon.

There's nothing wrong with being rejected. In fact, it helps you eliminate one option and move onto the next. When one door closes, another one opens—you just have to look hard enough.

FOCUS ON THE GOAL

Your goal is a crucial factor in keeping you motivated. If you have a clear desire and idea about where you want to go, then a reminder about your goal will lift you back up and tell you to keep moving.

Sara Bareilles's single goal was to get the attention of a major record label. Although she was invited to a series of private performances, where she would play a few songs live, they all ended up in rejection.

"The rejections kept coming until 'no' became the answer I expected." She felt like giving up.

If becoming a singer is your goal and you were told your songs weren't good, your sound wasn't fresh, and your style was terrible, you might quickly lose motivation. But she didn't.

What kept her going was the focus on her goal.

She had a few fans and continued to play at shows and perform at her very best. In the face of any rejection, she kept going on stage. Even while working as a waitress to make ends meet, she played gigs on the side to pay for rehearsal spaces.

She sang anywhere and everywhere. It wouldn't matter how many people turned up. Because of her perseverance, it so happened that at one of her small gigs, a rep was there who would sign Bareilles to a record deal.

"Life is a big, long free fall," Bareilles reflected, "and the sooner you can embrace what is beautiful about that, the sooner you will start to enjoy the ride."

Bareilles remained focused on her goals. Much like Howard Shultz in growing Starbucks and J.K. Rowling in publishing Harry Potter, the goal kept her moving forward, past the rejections.

Rejection is a prevalent theme among writers. Stephen King and William Golding have written fantastic books, but at one time, they were all rejected. Yet they continued to write.

Singers continue to perform. Comedians keep trying to make people laugh.

With a very sharp focus, rejection becomes a part of the process and no longer something that demotivates you. When in doubt, focus on your goal.

REJECTION HELPS FIND WHAT YOU WERE MEANT FOR

Rejection is a way for you to find what you want. When Steve Jobs was thrown out of Apple, he took it as an opportunity for growth.

"I didn't see it then, but it turned out that getting fired from Apple was the best thing that could ever happen to me."

He would go on to found a software company, NeXT, and bought a small animation studio called Pixar. These were what made his first billion dollars.

When he returned to Apple, he would turn the company around, and the rest is history.

"You can't connect the dots looking forward; you can only connect them looking backward. So, you have to trust that the dots will somehow connect in your future."

For Jobs, rejection directed him to where he needed to head and gave him time to improve and work on himself.

Rejection gives you time to self-reflect.

Heroes see rejection as a point of growth or a test to determine how much they want something.

Jeff Bezos had difficulty raising money for Amazon, taking sixty meetings to raise $1 million.

Elon Musk, in his attempt to build an aerospace business, made a deal with Russian companies that kept refusing to sell him rockets. Because of this rejection he put the venture off and went on to build Zip2—which would be his first big success. Ironically, he would then go on to create SpaceX and now makes his own rockets.

With each rejection, you move closer to what you are meant to do. The faster you get rejected, the faster you find what you want.

If you were fourteen, became pregnant, and then lost your child, what would you do?

That's the start of Oprah Winfrey's story. She majored in communications and became an ABC affiliate in Baltimore.

Soon, she was hired as a primetime news co-anchor, and when she made her debut it failed. She was blamed for the failure, was demoted to writer, and told she shouldn't be there.

But she didn't give up. Rather than stay upset about the situation, she found her love for television there and then. She loved hosting and went in search of any job that would help get her started.

She took a job co-hosting a show called *People are Talking*. Although this was a "downgrade," the show ran successfully, which then allowed Oprah to be recruited as a host for a morning talk show.

That show would make the program, *Oprah*, and its host, become a household name.

How heroes respond to rejection is what makes them heroes.

Rejections aren't hard to remember. I remember the times I've been told I wasn't fit for the job. I wasn't good enough. I didn't have the skills.

One time, I remember sulking around for a month, wasting my time and doing absolutely nothing with my life. I could have easily picked up a language or applied for more jobs, but I didn't. I wasted time—time that I can't get back.

When you are rejected, remember you're moving forward like these heroes. It's a necessity. It's a part of your journey to helping you achieve your goal. It may still taste bitter, but it's necessary medicine.

Don't waste time doing nothing because the world keeps moving. Recover as quickly as possible, continually focusing on your goal. You have a mission. Otherwise, why did you set yourself on the path in the first place?

Steal your hero's tenacity. Move even when you are knocked down. In times when you are rejected, channel these heroes. Remember: Rejection helps you.

Rejection is a good thing.

21. IGNORE THE NOISE

Ignoring the noise is a difficult task. I have always found it challenging to determine what *is* noise. Is your friend trying to give you sound advice or simply dragging you down? Is the media wrong or right about your plan?

To say that heroes are immune to noise would certainly be wrong. It is tough to ignore a friend who is telling you to stop pursuing your business idea. It is hard to ignore your parents telling you to stop working on your dreams.

How can you decipher what critical feedback is? How can you know who is trying to pull you down?

Anything that prevents you from achieving your goal is noise.

Whatever you pursue—from running a marathon to becoming an astronaut—if someone tells you to stop doing it, they are merely slowing you down. They say it's a pipe dream. They may have their own personal reasons for saying this. They may think it's not suitable for you. Ignore them. If you're set on something, pursue it to the end.

Noise is just slowing you down. Why delay achievement?

BE CAREFUL OF THE NOISE CLOSEST TO YOU

Some of your closest relationships can become noise.

A good friend of mine sat with me at a café while we were talking about our future plans. My app development company was growing and started to make money.

I told him of the growth and the first thing he said, "No, you aren't. Stop pretending."

I was visibly shocked. I could have pulled the papers out and shown him the money coming in. I could have taken out app reviews, but I was in disbelief.

My own friend was trying to tell me to stop. I realized that he no longer supported my goal. I told him it was real and he immediately repeated that I was lying.

He had become noise.

A few years have passed since that moment, and I won't forget it. People can become noise when they see you start to succeed. Ignore them.

Heroes do eventually figure out what they should or shouldn't listen to. In doing so, they can concentrate on what is truly helping them achieve their goals, and what isn't. By filtering noise out, they keep their minds clear of clutter. Information that isn't relevant or useful in their pursuits is filtered out.

WE DON'T THINK YOU CAN FLY

The Wright brothers were called liars. People never believed that they created a plane. Although they announced that they had done so in the desert, and even though some reporters saw it happen, no one really believed them.

The media accused them of lying. How could two boys who ran a bicycle shop make man-made flight possible? Others who were heavily funded, such as Sir Langley, were unable to find a solution, yet these two boys out of nowhere figured it out?

Impossible.

The Wright Brothers' journey was filled with noise. Everyone ridiculed them. When Wilbur Wright decided to fly and end the disbelief, a reporter who saw him after landing describes that eventful day, "I saw the man who is said to be unemotional turn pale. He had long suffered in silence; he was conscious that the world no longer doubted his achievements."

From that day onward, everything went in complete reversal. Numerous associations would congratulate them. Other inventors who were also in the race to build a plane said, "We are beaten."

The crowd was still against them, but they pursued. When Wilbur decided to showcase his skills and fly around the Statue of Liberty, he didn't brag, he just did it.

To silence the noise, you must show. You can't silence the noise until you force them to see it with their own eyes. Words will never be enough.

YOU CAN'T RUN

Similar to the Wright Brothers, Usain Bolt had to deal with the world disbelieving his record-breaking run. Bolt originally ran long distances, not the 100 meters for which he would become famous.

Although he was competitive in nature, he was sidetracked by noise multiple times. He fell prey to partying and got cocky, skipping classes to play games, only stopping when his cousin snitched on him.

It was when he saw his own hero, Michael Johnson, run that he wanted to be a gold medalist just like Johnson. He had a vision to be in the Olympics.

When he did start taking running seriously, he was booed many times. That was when his coach told him to run for himself and not the crowd. His new mantra was: *Don't think about them. Just do.*

It is no surprise then that in Jamaica, when he ran the 100m sprint, no one believed his record-breaking time of 9.76 seconds. The world denied it happened. They called him a liar. But that didn't stop him. He was going to show them.

Only six months later, he got that chance. Not only did he beat the proposed 9.76 seconds, but he also broke the world record. The commentators screamed into the microphone: "That is the *fastest* any *human* has ever covered 100 *meters*. Usain Bolt has run the fastest hundred meters in the *history of mankind!*"

His time? 9.72 seconds.

He destroyed the competition and kept silent until he had his chance to perform. He silenced his critics and the noise by showing what he could do.

YOU ARE THE MAN IN THE ARENA

There is a famous saying by Theodore Roosevelt: "It is not the critic who counts; not the man who points out how the strong man stumbles … The credit belongs to the man who is actually in the arena, whose face is marred by dust and sweat and blood."

This famous speech by Roosevelt, "The Man in the Arena," has been referenced a lot through history. Lebron James writes it on his shoes before a game. Nixon quoted it in his resignation speech. Nelson Mandela gave a copy to the captain of the South African rugby team, Francois Pienaar, before the start of the 1995 Rugby World Cup (the team won).

Who is it that Roosevelt refers to when he addresses the "man in the arena"? It is anyone who is pursuing what they want. It is easy for critics to criticize what you're doing. The crowds can quickly point to your failures or laugh in disbelief. Some may even enjoy pulling you down and jeering at your failed attempts (Andre Agassi had many opponents who tried to rub it in his face when he lost).

Heroes ignore these critics—if not in their relationships, then in their minds.

People will think they know what it is like to be in the arena, whether it be in your job or in your situation. It is far easier to be spectator than to be an actual participant.

I have found myself talking as if I were in the arena many times. When a colleague of mine was training for a triathlon, I gave him advice even though I had never been in one.

Another friend of mine was running a restaurant, and I was an idiot to give him guidance on how he should run it. It is so easy to pass judgment and critique what other people are doing.

Looking back, I can only imagine now how much stress these people were under: the financial pressures, the staffing problems, the physical efforts. I never put any of this into consideration. I just abused the man in the arena. I wasn't the one sweating it out.

No single hero was ever a critic, but they certainly have encountered them. No hero was the noise. Don't become the spectator throwing oranges or telling the man in the arena how to fight.

What you must steal from these heroes is the ability to ignore the critics.

You are the person in the arena. You are the person pursuing your goals and vision.

There will always be people who want to pull you down or pass judgment. Whatever their reason, you must ignore these people. *You're* the man in the arena. Your mind and time are finite.

Steal the ability to ignore the noise.

22. BE RESPECTFUL

I am guilty of treating people differently. I have been rude and didn't treat everyone with the same respect. When I make an investment in someone, it will, occasionally, come back to bite me. Once I threw myself into a friendship and ended up getting bullied by that very same person.

If *How to Win Friends and Influence People* has taught us anything, it's to treat people with respect. It might come as obvious advice, but we often forget this in times of stress or urgency.

We could be predisposed to hate someone before we even meet them, even if they have done us no wrong.

Heroes treat everyone with respect. In most cases, our heroes didn't get to where they are without the help of someone else. Their choice to be respectful allowed them to succeed.

THE PAYBACK THAT SAVED A COMPANY

Milton Hershey would have never succeeded if it weren't for a boy named Harry Lebkicher, nicknamed Lebbie. When Milton started his first company to sell candy with short poems written inside, he needed some help. Enter an eager boy named Lebbie, who worked at the lumberyard and loved having the opportunity to work with candy.

Even though the two occasionally argued about how the business was run, they formed a mutual respect. Although the company would fail a few years later, they enjoyed the experience. They would go their separate ways and it was unlikely they would meet again.

As it happens, they did.

After failing another company, Milton had finally figured out what he needed to do to succeed. He asked family members for money, but they refused to assist him. It was then that Milton decided to get in touch with his old friend and employee, Lebbie. Perhaps Lebbie believed that Milton would succeed and remembered the respect Milton had given him. He provided him a meal and a place to sleep for the night.

Milton had a dilemma regarding all his equipment that he had accumulated from his failed ventures. It was all locked away until a tax was paid. Lebbie came to the rescue and paid to have the equipment released.

It was here that Milton succeeded with his third venture, the Lancaster Caramel Company.

If Milton had not treated Lebbie with respect, there is little doubt that Lebbie would not have come to Milton's rescue. In fact, it would be fair to say that Hershey's chocolates might never have existed if it weren't for Lebbie.

Similar to investors or people who may be able to assist you in your time of need, if you don't give them respect, why would you expect them to help you?

Milton was never banking on Lebbie to bail him out, but at the time of need, Lebbie had to draw on something. And that was his memory of Milton's generosity and kindness.

THE INSIDER

Respect has a surprising way of paying you back.

Nike, for example, might not have been Nike today if it weren't for an inside man. Phil Knight, the founder, had traveled to Japan and met a man named Fujimoto. Fujimoto was working for Nike's shoe supplier, and a recent typhoon had destroyed his bike. Getting to work was difficult.

Knight realized this was a hard-working man and respected him. He sent him some money to buy a bicycle and never thought of it again.

But the company had fading relations with their Japanese supplier and things started to go downhill. The shoes were arriving late, the quality dropped, and communication seemed extremely difficult. Knight had no idea what was wrong or what was happening.

It so happens that Fujimoto decided to let Knight know that the supplier was trying to make a clean break. It no longer wanted to work with Nike, as it felt the relationship wasn't profitable and wished to sever ties as soon as possible.

Because Knight had this knowledge early, they formulated a plan and started to reorganize the company. They found their own manufacturers and started making their own shoes.

If it weren't for that extra information from Fujimoto, Nike might never have been born. Instead, it may have gone bankrupt. Knight, the CEO of the company, never expected any help from Fujimoto, an employee in a factory, but they were respectful toward each other.

Heroes don't expect to be paid back. They respect people; knowing respect will pay itself forward. And it's the people we often least expect who will remember our respect for them and possibly help us in the future. What is your lasting impression on someone?

You must have clear, positive intentions and be honest. This isn't about giving and taking. There are no expectations.

RESPECT BREEDS RESPECT

Respect is tough to build. But once you have it, it's invaluable. People will believe your words. They will look up to you. Only good things stem from being respectful to others.

When Kerry Stokes, a media mogul, was to meet David Gonski, who had just arrived at an airport, he didn't order a car to pick Gonski up. He could have. After all, Stokes was a wealthy man. But he had come from very humble beginnings. Growing up, he always treated people with kindness and respect so much so that when you asked anyone about him, responses were only kind words.

So, when Gonski arrived, Stokes himself was there to meet him.

"Stokes goes out of his way to include relative strangers, to make them feel wanted and on the team," Gonski reflected.

Gonski would become a life-long friend and adviser to Stokes. Meeting Gonski was a sign of respect and the kind of small token of appreciation that can only lead to a stronger connection. As a consequence, the two formulated multiple deals that led to success for both of them.

Heroes' stories are littered with these tales. In most cases, these actions impacted their success (and most of the time, they didn't even know it). It is a cliché, but the truth is this: The way that you treat people is the way *you* want to be treated.

"Respect," Richard Branson says, "is how to treat everyone, not just those you want to impress."

What Branson refers to is when he was looking for partners to take on a stake in his company, Virgin Music. He remembered some businessmen from Japan who had treated him kindly years ago for another business deal but had no money. He decided to contact them. They would strike a deal—all because they treated him with respect.

What we should steal from these heroes is respect for everyone.

Heroes are surrounded by the people they respect, and they return that respect in kind.

You may never know when someone will be able to help you or turn your fortunes around.

Hershey and Knight were only able to succeed because they respected the people they had met in their lives. Stokes and Branson always did business with respect, and consequently the people around them looked up to them with admiration.

Every day, when I meet a new face, I'm reminded that this is a person I may never meet again, but I want to make sure I leave a positive impression for them. That is the respect they deserve.

So, every day you meet someone, channel one of these heroes by showing respect and earning respect.

23. BECOME THE HERO

In this book, you learned about the different traits that helped heroes succeed.

In Part I, you prepared yourself for the journey ahead. You learned the secret to motivation: a strong belief. J.K. Rowling had an unwavering belief in Harry Potter, and in the face of rejections she continued to write and finished her book.

> *Belief is the one element that will keep you motivated when you're at rock bottom.*

When heroes did fail, they realized that failure was a lesson. Walt Disney had a series of failures before he succeeded. But each time he fell, he stood back up, brushed himself off, and worked toward his dreams.

> *Failure is a learning curve for heroes, not a dead-end.*

You saw the heroes that took ownership of their lives and, consequently, took control of their future. Jocko Willink was willing to own up to his mistakes even if he lost his job, which allowed him to create successful Navy teams in the future.

> *At all times you must take ownership. You must be willing to risk it all.*

You learned of Doyle Brunson who may have been a very successful sports star, but his dreams were crushed by an accident. His cards were dealt; and he played with what he had in his hand.

Reality can be painful, but concentrating on the negatives or the constraints can genuinely prevent you from achieving your goals.

You also saw Marilyn Monroe change from a rejected model to a successful actor. She changed her beliefs from within and that lead to her success.

Whatever the goal, whatever the change. it's possible—and it starts with you.

In Part II, you begin the journey of achieving your goals. You learned of Stephen King's wife, Tabby, who was integral to his success. His first successful book was published because Tabby found his manuscript in the rubbish bin. She encouraged him to finish the book. The people around you matter, so spend time with those that will help you on your journey.

Be selective about the people you hang around and share your goals with. They will be the people who will want your success, no matter what.

While you're on the path to success, you must be constantly learning. Time is a finite resource. Whatever you need to learn, learn well and deliberately.

Learning is an essential component to success, and every single hero pursues it in every field related to their goal.

In pursuit of your goals, don't fall for the fairy tale of pursuing your passion. Work first on your inclinations, like P.T. Barnum or Felix Dennis. Then you will have all the time in the world to work on your passions.

You don't have to quit your day job. You don't have to make your passion your job. Work on your inclinations first.

But remain curious. Always be willing to try new things like Ray Kroc and Howard Shultz, who founded solid businesses because they stayed curious.

Don't let your curiosity go unanswered.

And if an opportunity does come by, remember Tina Fey, who found her success by saying yes to any opportunity.

You shouldn't aimlessly say yes. Instead, say yes to real opportunity and not because you think it will make someone else happy.

When you set your goals, be concise about what they are and how you plan to get there. Bear Grylls and Benjamin Franklin did not achieve their goals without a clear plan.

Clear goals and a clear plan are necessary to achieve what you want.

But don't get sidetracked along the way. Stick to one goal. Like Milton Hershey or Kevin Hart, you can only achieve success by diving deep into your *one thing*.

By sticking to one thing, you can see it to the end and perfect it.

In Part III, you learned about the obstacles that may hinder your progress to success. No journey will be smooth sailing. Don't hold onto grudges because they may prevent you from concentrating on the benefits and distract you from your goals.

Concentrate on the goal and tasks at hand. Use your energy toward creating a new plan for new successes.

Ignore the people who are pulling you down. Surround yourself with supporters and people who actually want to see you succeed. Remember the Wright Brothers.

To silence the noise, you must show your success. You can't silence the noise until you force them to see your achievement with their own eyes. Words will never be enough.

And finally, don't ever fear rejection. It's part of the process.

By actively being open to rejection, you may gain perspectives to open new paths for you. Rejection is a positive experience that comes from being openly curious.

So, picture the person you want to be. Do you want to have crowds looking up to you? Maybe you'll be happy with just your family respecting your achievements. Perhaps you want to look into the mirror and be proud of who you are.

Create the hero you want to be. Find the traits you need. Set off on your journey.

Make a list of your hero's traits and learn their stories. Model yourself off them. Create your *own* stories. Make your *own* mistakes. Learn your *own* lessons.

When you find yourself at crossroads or unsure of what to do, ask yourself what your hero would do. Channel them and remind yourself of their choices. Then move forward. Do *not* stand still. No hero stood still.

Like all heroes, you must be persistent and dedicated to your goal. Steal the traits that matter most to you and prioritize them. There is no wrong or right. The only wrong you can do is to not continually work on yourself. Sooner or later, you will become the hero for someone else.

I'm reminded every day that people become heroes by pursuing their goals and dreams. When I had an idea, I just dove in to try to make it happen.

One idea was simple: a map application that showed everyone where to park for free. Why wouldn't someone pay $5 for an app that saved them money?

After four months of walking around the city, marking the free parking spots on the app, I taught myself programming. I released the app with only three sales. But at that time, the lack of sales didn't matter to me because I had revealed a problem. I had found a solution. And I had made the app.

That momentum threw me into believing that I could achieve whatever I want so long as I put my mind to it.

When I tried to make a game company, it didn't succeed for more than four years. I kept putting money into it, hoping for a return. I reminded myself that many entrepreneurs were in the negative before their company succeeded. I kept telling myself that if these heroes are willing to live off cans of tuna and ramen, so would I (which I did).

Eventually, we did create a hit virtual reality game (Crazy Fishing VR), which helped turn the company around.

Even though my story has failures, I realize that they define me as much as my successes. When I look back, much like any hero looking back on their own journey, I realize I am creating a story.

Your story is what matters and every story needs a hero.

That hero is you.

So, go on, hero…

Make your story.

Acknowledgements

To write a book takes a long time. Without the amazing people around me I would have never finished this one.

To Jenny, for supporting me through this endeavor. Thank you.

To Maria and Barry, thank you for guiding me along this wonderful journey of writing and editing.

To my family, thank you for believing in me.

To my friends who believe I am capable of more, you are awesome.

And finally, to my supporters, whether it be on social media or in real life—you made this possible. Without you, I could never have been confident enough to release this book. Thank you.

Bibliography

Abraham Lincoln
Donald, D. H. 1996. *Lincoln.* 1st ed. New York: Touchstone.

Andrew Hallam
Hallam, A. 2011. *Millionaire Teacher: The Nine Rules of Wealth You Should Have Learned in School.* Hoboken, New Jersey: Wiley.

Arnold Schwarzenegger
Schwarzenegger, A., & Petre, P. 2012. *Total Recall: My Unbelievably True Life Story.* 1st ed. New York: Simon & Schuster.

Ben Carson
Carson, B., & Murphey, C. 1990. *Gifted Hands.* Grand Rapids, Michigan: Zondervan Books.

Ben Horowitz
Horowitz, B. 2014. *The Hard Thing About Hard Things: Building a Business When There Are No Easy Answers.* 1st ed. New York: Harper Business.

Benjamin Franklin
Franklin, B. 2006. *The Autobiography of Benjamin Franklin.* NuVision Publications.

Bob Iger
Iger, R. 2019. *The Ride of a Lifetime: Lessons Learned from 15 Years as CEO of the Walt Disney Company*. 1st ed. New York: Random House.

Chris Hadfield
Hadfield, C. 2013. *An Astronaut's Guide to Life on Earth*. 1st ed. New York: Little, Brown and Company.

Daymond John
John, D., & Paisner, D. 2016. *The Power of Broke: how empty pockets, a tight budget, and a hunger for success can become your greatest competitive advantage*. 1st ed. New York: Crown Business.

Derek Sivers
Sivers, D. 2015. *Anything You Want: 40 Lessons for a New Kind of Entrepreneur*. Portfolio/Penguin edition. New York: Portfolio/Penguin.

Doyle Brunson
Brunson, D. 2009. *The Godfather of Poker: The Doyle Brunson Story*. 1st ed. Cardoza.

Dr. Seuss
Jones, B. J. 2019. *Becoming Dr. Seuss: Theodor Geisel and the making of an American imagination*. New York: Dutton.

Ed Catmull
Catmull, E., & Wallace, A. 2014. *Creativity, Inc.: Overcoming the Unseen Forces That Stand in the Way of True Inspiration*. 1st ed. New York: Random House.

Felix Baumgartner
Lynch, K. 2013. *Mission to the Edge of Space: The Full Story Behind Red Bull Stratos*. Film.

Felix Dennis
Dennis, F. 2008. *How to Get Rich: One of the World's Greatest Entrepreneurs Shares His Success Wisdom.* 1st American ed. New York: Portfolio.

Gary Keller
Keller, G., & Papasan, J. 2012. *The One Thing: The Surprisingly Simple Truth Behind Extraordinary Results.* Austin, Texas: Bard Press.

Helen Keller
Keller, H. 1954. *The Story of My Life.* Garden City, New York: Doubleday.

Henry Ford
Ford, H., & Crowther, S. 1973. *My Life and Work.* New York: Arno Press.

Howard Schultz
Schultz, H. 2012. *Pour Your Heart Into It.* New York: Hachette Books.

Jack Ma
Clark, D. 2016. *Alibaba: The House That Jack Ma Built.* 1st ed. New York: Ecco Press.

James Caan
Caan, J. 2010. *The Real Deal James Caan.* UK, Virgin Digital.

Jan Arnold, Bill Klein
Arnold, J., & Klein, B. 2015. *Life is Short (no pun intended): Love, Laughter, and Learning to Enjoy Every Moment.* New York: Howard Books, imprint of Simon & Schuster, Inc.

Jerry Weintraub
Weintraub, J., & Cohen, R. 2010. *When I Stop Talking, You'll Know I'm Dead: Useful Stories From a Persuasive Man.* New York: Twelve.

Jia Jiang
Jiang, J. 2015. *Rejection Proof: How I Beat Fear and Became Invincible Through 100 Days of Rejection*. 1st ed. New York: Harmony.

Jocko Willink
Willink, J., & Babin, L. 2017. *Extreme Ownership: How U.S. Navy SEALs Lead and Win*. 2nd ed. New York: St. Martin's Press.

J.R.R. Tolkien
Shippey, T. A. 2002. *J.R.R. Tolkien: Author of the Century*. 1st ed. Houghton Mifflin. Boston: Houghton Mifflin.

Kerry Stokes
Rule, A. 2015. *Kerry Stokes: The Bow From Nowhere*. 1st ed. HarperCollins Publishers Pty Ltd.

Kevin Hart
Hart, K., & Strauss, N. 2017. *I Can't Make This Up: Life Lessons*. 1st ed. 37 INK/Atria Books.

Kobe Bryant
McHugh, A. 2001. *Kobe Bryant*. Chanhassen, MN: Child's World.

Marilyn Monroe
Leaming, B. 2000. *Marilyn Monroe*. New York: Three Rivers Press.

Marc Cuban
Cuban, M. 2011. *How to Win at the Sport of Business*. New York: Diversion Books.

Michael Dell
Dell, M., & Fredman, C. 1999. *Direct from Dell: Strategies That Revolutionized an Industry*. New York: Harper Business.

Michael Jordan
Lazenby, R. 2014. *Michael Jordan: the Life*. 1st ed. New York: Little, Brown and Company.

Milton Hershey
Malone, M. and Hutchinson, W. 1971. *Milton Hershey, Chocolate King*. Champaign, Illinois: Garrard Pub. Co.

Muhammad Ali
Eig, J. 2017. *Ali: A Life*. Boston: Houghton Mifflin Harcourt.

Nikola Tesla
Carlson, W. B. 2013. *Tesla: Inventor of the Electrical Age*. Princeton, New Jersey: Princeton University Press.

Oprah Winfrey
Kelley, K. 2010. *Oprah: A Biography*. New York: Crown.

P.T. Barnum
Barnum, P. T. 1., & Browne, W. R. 1. 1972. *Barnum's Own Story*. P. Smith.

Ray Kroc
Kroc, R. 1977. *Grinding It Out: The Making of McDonald's*. Chicago: H. Regnery.

Richard Branson
Branson, R. 1998. *Losing My Virginity: How I've Had Fun and Made a Fortune Doing Business My Way*. New York: Times Business.

Sal Khan
Khan, S. 2012. *The One World Schoolhouse: Education Reimagined*. New York: Twelve.

Sam Walton
Walton, S., & Huey, J. 1992. *Sam Walton, Made in America: My Story.* New York: Doubleday.

Samuel Zemurray
Cohen, R. 2012. *The Fish That Ate the Whale: The Life and Times of America's Banana King.* New York: Farrar, Straus & Giroux.

Sara Bareilles
Bareilles, S. 2015. *Sounds Like Me: My Life (so far) In Song.* 1st ed. New York: Simon & Schuster.

Soichiro Honda
Murray, J. 2018. *Honda.* Minneapolis, Minnesota: Abdo Zoom.

Stephen King
King, S. 2010. *On Writing: A Memoir of the Craft.* Scribner trade. New York, NY: Scribner.

Steve Jobs
Isaacson, W. 2013. *Steve Jobs.* 1st ed. New York: Simon & Schuster.

Theodore Roosevelt
McCullough, D. G. 2003. *Mornings On Horseback.* New York: Simon and Schuster.

Tina Fey
Fey, T. 2011. *Bossypants.* New York: Little, Brown and Co.

Usain Bolt
Bolt, U. 2014. *Usain Bolt: Faster Than Lightning. My Story.* Great Britain: HarperCollins Publishers.

Rafa Nadal
Nadal, R. and Carlin, J. 2012. *Rafa*. London: Sphere.

Walt Disney
Miller, D. and Martin, P. 2005. *The Story of Walt Disney*. New York: Disney Editions.

Warren Buffet
Schroeder, A. 2008. *The Snowball: Warren Buffett and the Business of Life*. New York: Bantam Books.

Wright Brothers
McCullough, D. G. 2015. *The Wright Brothers*. Simon & Schuster.

www.ingramcontent.com/pod-product-compliance
Lightning Source LLC
Chambersburg PA
CBHW020326010526
44107CB00054B/1993